The New Right

V.

T

DEMCO

The New Right
V.
The Constitution

Stephen Macedo

Library of Congress Cataloging-in-Publication Data

Macedo, Stephen, 1957–
  The New Right v. the Constitution.

  Includes bibliographical references.
  1. United States—Constitutional law—Interpretation
and construction.   2. Conservatism—United States.
I. Title.
KF4550.M22   1986   342.73'029   86-14763
ISBN 0-932790-59-3 (pbk.)   347.30229

Printed in the United States of America.

CATO INSTITUTE
224 Second Street SE
Washington, D.C. 20003

For D. G.

The strength of the Courts of law has always been the greatest security that can be offered to personal independence; but this is more especially the case in democratic ages. Private rights and interests are in constant danger if the judicial power does not grow more extensive and stronger to keep pace with equality of conditions.

—Alexis de Tocqueville
Democracy in America

Contents

FOREWORD
Richard A. Epstein   xi

  I. INTRODUCTION   1

 II. THE FRAMERS OF THE CONSTITUTION v. JUDGE BORK   5

III. THE MAJORITARIAN MYTH   21

IV. MORALITY AND CONSTITUTIONAL LAW   33

 V. PRINCIPLED JUDICIAL ACTIVISM   43

VI. LIBERTY AND COMMUNITY   51

VII. CONCLUSION   57

Foreword

Stephen Macedo's monograph *The New Right v. the Constitution* contains a number of constitutional ironies. For decades, liberals and conservatives have been divided over the proper approach to constitutional interpretation. The standard liberal view has emphasized the openness of the constitutional text and the need to take changed circumstances into account in construing constitutional provisions. Liberated from the confining notion of Original Intent, judicial activism in support of fundamental values became the centerpiece of the liberal agenda. It culminated in the Supreme Court's most important decision, *Brown* v. *Board of Education*, which ordered the end of de jure segregation in public schools, and, far more controversially, in *Roe* v. *Wade*, which constitutionalized women's right to abortion.

The conservatives have observed a different set of principles. In their view, the Constitution primarily established the rules for the operation of democratic institutions. The structural provisions of the Constitution thus dominate provisions intended to secure individual rights against the government. A presumption of judicial restraint was the result of this fundamental position.

Macedo's essay is yet further evidence that the straightforward dichotomy between left and right, liberal and conservative, is now breaking down. Macedo is to be commended for bringing the libertarian, natural-rights tradition back to constitutional interpretation. He launches a sustained attack on three basic conservative tenets: the doctrine of Original Intent, which holds that the Constitution should be interpreted in accordance with the intentions of the Framers who drafted and ratified it; the assumption that the Constitution organized a system of popular democracy; and the view of judicial restraint that is said to follow from these two positions. For Macedo, the limitations upon popular democracy are as much a part of the Constitution as the institutions of democracy itself. Accordingly, judges cannot indulge the easy presumption that legislation is constitutional unless the contrary is clearly shown. Instead, in each case there has to be a neutral inquiry into how the provisions of a statute square with the language and structure of the Constitution. The invalidation of legislation is not some extraordinary event in the life of a constitutional democracy; it is part of the original design.

The target of Macedo's attack is noted conservative Robert Bork, now on the circuit court for the District of Columbia and frequently mentioned as a possible Reagan candidate for a future vacancy on the Supreme Court. Macedo also criticizes Attorney General Edwin Meese and Assistant Attorney General for Civil Rights Bradford Reynolds.

Macedo is clearly correct in rejecting the idea that the Constitution envisions an unfettered system of popular democracy: the provisions protecting individual rights are entitled to a dignity equal to that of other parts of the Constitution. Although Macedo does not emphasize the point, I am persuaded that the dangers of faction demonstrate the wisdom of entrenching individual rights against the state. The common perception that "special interests" are able to take over the legislature is all too true. The fear of faction in turn raises concerns as to both substance and process. Special-interest legislation, for example, can direct government expenditures to a single group out of general revenues, and it can exempt certain groups from taxation. In each case, the unequal distribution of benefits and burdens is rightly perceived as fundamentally unfair. An elaborate effort to take from A and give to B, such legislation is an appropriate subject for judicial review.*

I would also argue, with Macedo, that one has to be very cautious in dealing with the question of "specific intent." Both he and Justice Brennan are correct in insisting that it is fruitless to interpret the general provisions of the Constitution solely with reference to the particular legislative abuses that prompted their passage. Macedo demonstrates anew how circumstances can undermine a theory of specific intent, understood as an effort to seek out the motivations of the Framers. He shows with great vigor the difficulties of ascertaining "the" constitutional intent when all that is available in the record is the inconsistent, ambiguous, and unreflective intentions of the large group of independent persons who participated in drafting or ratifying the Constitution. In this respect, the search for

---

*My book *Takings: Private Property and the Power of Eminent Domain* discusses the legal principles on which that review of taxation and other forms of government action should be undertaken.

constitutional intent is no simpler than the more routine search for contractual intent in complex multiparty-contract cases.

The jurisprudential concern with intention has another, more useful side, one that should not be discarded along with the vain quest for Original Intent. The invocation of intent can stand for the position that the text of the Constitution has to be the sole source of judicial authority, for if the text cannot constrain unelected judges, then very little else can. Often it is useful to assume that the Constitution means precisely what it says, that the reason the Constitution protects freedom of speech or private property, for example, is that it says so. The text then provides the basis for a sustained analysis of the original provisions, which, as Macedo well understands, need not produce a crabbed or narrow interpretation. This theory of textual intent, moreover, places significant limitations upon the power of the courts to do what they will. Bork, Meese, and Reynolds may be vulnerable insofar as they indicate a dominant role for popular democracy, but they are correct insofar as they rule out the idea of a "living Constitution" that allows judges to disregard the specific text while searching for the contemporary underlying values of constitutional discourse.

Without sound, textually based constitutional interpretation, the shape of the law becomes subject to competing value preferences. Macedo quotes Justice Brennan's well-known Georgetown speech to the effect that a theory of "specific" intent is an inadequate guide to constitutional interpretation. But Brennan's alternative, his vision of an evolving Constitution, cannot itself withstand scrutiny against a more traditional textual approach. As Macedo points out, Brennan and other liberal thinkers either ignore or downplay property rights firmly grounded in the Constitution's text. Elsewhere in his speech, Brennan insists that the cause of "human dignity" is so powerful that the cruel-and-unusual-punishment provision of the Eighth Amendment should be read as imposing a total and absolute prohibition on the death penalty. This position, however, is flatly inconsistent with the constitutional text. The Fifth Amendment, passed at the same time as the Eighth, expressly states, "No person shall be held to answer for a *capital*, or otherwise infamous crime, unless on a present or indictment of a Grand Jury . . . nor shall any person be subject for the same offense to be twice put in jeopardy of *life* or limb; nor shall he be deprived of *life*, liberty, or property, without due process of law" (emphasis added). The three distinct references to the death penalty rule out the idea that the cruel-and-unusual-punishment clause of the Eighth Amendment bans the death penalty in its entirety. To allow a theory of an evolving constitution to undermine the text is to substitute naked value preferences for law, the abuse traditional conservatives have so long condemned. It is also an exceedingly dangerous practice because once it begins, it cannot be restrained. If one were to argue, for example, that advances in penology and incarceration make the death penalty inappropriate, then someone else could argue that the rapid increase in the crime rate makes the use of torture appropriate, notwithstanding the constitutional prohibition on cruel and unusual punishment.

On the other hand, it is a far harder question whether the cruel-and-unusual-punishment clause imposes any restriction on the invocation of the death penalty in *some* circumstances. That question is troublesome for any theory of interpretation. Constitutions, like well-drafted contracts, limit the domain of permissible choice, but they do not dictate the outcome in all cases. We need, therefore, some sense of the implicit background assumptions against which the Constitution was drafted in order to apply its provisions to the questions that arise over time. It is here that Macedo's libertarian, natural-rights orientation should prove most instructive. Because the Constitution was drafted in the natural-rights, limited-government tradition, modern commentators in that tradition will be among those best able to explicate the principles that make the document so great and enduring a human achievement. Macedo's excellent essay is an important contribution to putting constitutional interpretation back on a sound basis, one capable of sustaining the liberties that are the singular virtue of our republic.

RICHARD A. EPSTEIN

University of Chicago Law School

I. Introduction

The rise to power of the New Right is the preeminent political phenomenon of the last decade. Not only have victories been won on tax cuts, domestic-spending cuts, and military-spending increases, but the political agenda itself has shifted in accordance with New Right imperatives. The waxing power of the right is, at the moment, most evident in the White House and the Senate. But whatever happens in the next election, New Right judicial appointees to the federal bench, and those who may yet join Justice Sandra Day O'Connor on the Supreme Court, will influence law and public policy in the United States for decades to come.

In the field of constitutional law, partisans of the New Right advocate a new majoritarianism and a fundamental narrowing of judicial protections for individual rights. The New Right's constitutional vision, if accepted by the nation's courts, would represent a decisive shift of power to legislative majorities and a basic revision of the nature of citizenship in America. A careful examination of the jurisprudence of the New Right is, therefore, in order.

The partisans of the New Right portray their constitutional vision as the culmination of hallowed tradition: they claim to be the ideological heirs of the Founding Fathers and the standard-bearers of the "historical constitution." But the New Right's claim to the Founders' legacy is dubious, its allegiance to the Constitution largely rhetorical, and its stature in relation to the great tradition of American constitutional thought unimpressive. What is striking, in fact, is how far the New Right has departed from the ideas of the Founders, the majestic phrases of the Constitution, and what is best in the American political tradition.

Political movements are not monolithic, and no brief work could encompass all the constitutional arguments of everyone associated with the New Right. The discussion in this book, therefore, focuses on a set of claims advanced by prominent New Right scholars and politicians—claims that together constitute the most distinctive and important features of the New Right's jurisprudence. For the sake of simplicity and clarity, the discussion concentrates on the jurisprudence of Judge Robert H. Bork, who has articulated the New Right's most important claims boldly and without inhibition.

It is with good reason that Judge Bork has come to be regarded as the foremost proponent of the constitutional theories of the New Right. As solicitor general, Bork gained national attention when, following the resignation of Attorney General Elliot L. Richardson and Deputy Attorney General William D. Ruckelshaus, he fired Archibald Cox, the special prosecutor in the Watergate affair. President Reagan has recognized Bork's stature by appointing him, along with fellow conservative law professors Richard A. Posner and Antonin Scalia, to the U.S. Court of Appeals. Bork is quoted approvingly in speeches by Attorney General Edwin Meese III, and he has been scathingly attacked in the pages of the *New York Review of Books* by the foremost constitutional scholar of the left as "Reagan's Justice."[1] And now, the name most often appearing on lists of likely Reagan Supreme Court nominations is Robert Bork.

It is not only Bork's notoriety but also his intellectual stature that makes him a formidable figure on the contemporary legal scene. Bork's assault on the active judicial protection of individual rights draws on the strongest and most often used weapons in the conservative armory.

First, partisans of the New Right profess a reverence for the "historical constitution" and argue that judges should adhere not simply to the text of the Constitution, but to the text interpreted in light of the specific intentions of its Framers. "It is necessary to establish the proposition," says Bork, "that the framers' intentions with respect to freedoms are the sole legitimate premise from which constitutional analysis may proceed."[2] The New Right is particularly skeptical about the broad rights to privacy and free speech that liberal judges claim to have discovered in the Constitution. Lino Graglia, a likely Reagan administration appointee to the federal bench, denies that the Framers were much concerned with liberty and asserts, "The Constitution's protections of individual rights are

---

[1]See Edwin Meese's addresses before the American Enterprise Institute (September 6, 1985) and the District of Columbia chapter of the Federalist Society Lawyers Division (November 15, 1985), copies of which may be obtained from the U.S. Department of Justice. See also Ronald Dworkin, "Reagan's Justice," *New York Review of Books*, November 8, 1984, pp. 27–31.

[2]Robert H. Bork, *Tradition and Morality in Constitutional Law*, Francis Boyer Lectures on Public Policy (Washington: American Enterprise Institute, 1984), p. 10.

not only few but also, when read in historical context, fairly clear and definite."[3]

Second, to circumscribe judicial power, conservatives argue that democracy is the basic constitutional value: "The original Constitution," according to Bork, "was devoted primarily to the mechanisms of democratic choice. . . . The makers of our Constitution . . . provided wide powers to representative assemblies and ruled only a few subjects off limits by the Constitution."[4] Giving majorities the power to pass laws defining how everyone should live is, says Bork, the "major freedom, of our kind of society." And Assistant Attorney General William Bradford Reynolds adds, "It was well understood at the American Founding that all governmental power derived from the people. Nothing other than popular sovereignty could comport . . . with the principles of the Revolution."[5] In construing individual rights broadly, say the partisans of the New Right, willful judges usurp matters that are properly legislative.

Third, the New Right claims that "abstract philosophical principles," which are often invoked to support rights claims, should have no authority in politics. For the conservatives, authority resides in the text of the Constitution interpreted in light of the specific historical intentions of the Framers, in democratic principles, and in the "common sense" of the people. Bork, moved by a deep moral skepticism, claims that moral ideas reflect only arbitrary, subjective preferences. Therefore, such "philosophical abstractions" as individual rights should be banished from our political discourse: they dress up and obscure the mere preferences of intellectuals, which deserve no special weight. Political majorities have, according to Bork, the right to define and "suppress" moral harms even if doing so thwarts what some people take to be individual rights or liberty.[6] Similarly, Reynolds derides "the political liberalism of the upper middle class, the university- and professional-school educated . . .

[3]Lino Graglia, "How the Constitution Disappeared," *Commentary* (February 1986):23. See also idem, "Would the Court Get 'Procedural Due Process' Cases Right If It Knew What 'Liberty' Really Means?" *Notre Dame Journal of Law, Ethics and Public Policy* 1 (1985):813–28. Graglia's position parallels Bork's.

[4]Bork, p. 9.

[5]William Bradford Reynolds, "Reviewing the American Constitutional Heritage," *Harvard Journal of Law and Public Policy* 8 (1985):226.

[6]Bork, p. 3.

the liberalism of a verbal elite . . . out of touch with the mass of Americans today."[7] And for Bork, to require toleration of diversity is to impose moral relativism and to provoke popular "weariness with turmoil and relativism."[8]

Fourth, the New Right asserts that requiring majority respect for minority rights privatizes morality, imposes moral relativism on society, and prevents the formation of a real community. Both Bork and Meese approvingly quote the conservative British jurist Lord Devlin: "What makes a society is a community of ideas, not political ideas alone but also ideas about the way its members should behave and govern their lives."[9]

All four components of the constitutional vision of the New Right, it is argued here, are faulty. References to original intentions do not settle hard constitutional issues. The Constitution does not set up a basically democratic scheme of government but rather a constitutional democracy, a scheme of limited government. Bork's moral skepticism is wholly unconvincing and deeply at odds with the constitutional text and our political traditions: these sources support an active judicial defense of a broad sphere of individual liberties. Liberty and community, finally, are not opposed: a society of free, tolerant individuals is the best form of community, a moral community comporting with America's heritage and the values enshrined in the Constitution. In sum, the New Right invokes "original intentions" in order to evade the only intentions that really count: the purposes embodied in the Constitution itself. The New Right's narrow interpretation of individual rights is supported not by the Constitution but by an ideology of majoritarianism and moral skepticism that is deeply at odds with the Constitution. Against both the New Right and the selective activists of the left, a principled activism in service of individual rights both personal and economic will be urged in these pages. By fusing constitutional interpretation and moral theory, principled activism vindicates the Constitution's authority by establishing its rightness.

[7]Reynolds, p. 234.
[8]Bork, p. 8.
[9]Ibid., p. 4; Meese, AEI address, pp. 10–11.

II. The Framers of the Constitution v. Judge Bork

Invocation of the intent of the Framers of the Constitution has long been a crucial element in the conservative attack on an active judiciary. Bork is unequivocal: "The framers' intentions with respect to freedoms are the sole legitimate premise from which constitutional analysis may proceed."[10] Activist judges, say conservatives, willfully ignore the intentions of the Framers, insert their own preferences into the Constitution, and in doing so perpetrate "limited coups d'etat."[11]

The invocation of the Framers' intentions has great political appeal. Attorney General Edwin Meese has now made it the ceterpiece of the Reagan administration's jurisprudence:

> What, then, should a constitutional jurisprudence actually be? It should be a Jurisprudence of Original Intention. . . . This belief in a Jurisprudence of Original Intention . . . reflects a deeply rooted commitment to the idea of democracy. . . . It has been and will continue to be the policy of this administration to press for a Jurisprudence of Original Intention. In the cases we file and those we join as *amicus*, we will endeavor to resurrect the original meaning of constitutional provisions and statutes as the only reliable guide for judgment.[12]

If every phrase in the Constitution were as easy to interpret as "neither shall any Person be eligible to that Office [the Presidency] who shall not have attained the Age of thirty five Years," enforcing its provisions would be an almost mechanical process. But even the First Amendment, whose words appear to speak plainly ("Congress shall make no law . . . abridging freedom of speech, or of the press")

---

[10]Bork, p. 10.

[11]Robert H. Bork, "Neutral Principles and Some First Amendment Problems," *Indiana Law Journal* 47(1971):6.

[12]Edwin Meese III, address before the American Bar Association, July 19, 1985, p. 15. Copies may be obtained from the U.S. Department of Justice.

raises extremely difficult problems of interpretation. The Constitution places a high value, if not the highest value, on democratic accountability, and so we can be confident that part of the purpose of the constitutional guarantee of free speech is to protect free and open debate on political matters. The First Amendment also protects, after all, the rights "to assemble, and to petition the Government for a redress of grievances." When the text of the Constitution is uncertain, help can be sought in the overall structure of the document, the relation between its various parts, or in the nature of the institutions the Constitution establishes. From this more general examination, we can conclude that the First Amendment certainly must protect political speech.

But certain forms of political speech may conflict with government's most basic purposes, such as the maintenance of national security and public order. There are some clear cases: for example, while citizens have a constitutionally protected right to criticize the government (although even that was not always obvious, witness the Alien and Sedition Acts), they do not have a right to publicize the sailing times of troop ships during wartime. But between the easy cases lie many hard ones: Do people have a right to oppose the constitutional order itself? Can people advocate forcible overthrow of the government? Can scholars publish and professors teach doctrines that public authorities consider dangerous to the established order?

Of course, the First Amendment does not specify that only political speech is to be protected; it says simply "speech." But what does "speech" include? Words that offend or libel? Words that some find obscene? Printed material that a majority of the community considers pornographic? Can sleeping in a public park or exotic dancing be forms of symbolic speech? Is corporate advertising a form of speech? In deciding these hard cases, judges have to articulate the basic principles and fundamental values that give substance and specificity to broad constitutional guarantees like the First Amendment.

The many difficult questions raised by the First Amendment are also extremely important. Although particular cases may affect only a handful of people, the principles articulated and applied by the Supreme Court and lower courts help determine the powers of legislative majorities and the rights of minorities. These rights and principles often become part of our political culture, determining in part the sort of regime we live under and the kind of people we become.

While the First Amendment raises a host of difficult issues, it is relatively straightforward compared with the truly majestic generalities that must also be interpreted and applied by judges. Witness the expansive phrasing of the Fourteenth Amendment:

> No State shall make or enforce any law which shall abridge the privileges or immunities of citizens of the United States; nor shall any State deprive any person of life, liberty or property, without due process of law; nor deny to any person within its jurisdiction the equal protection of the laws.

It is no easy matter to decide what these important phrases require, and here the Constitution's structure provides some assistance. Since 1925, the Supreme Court has given substance to the Fourteenth Amendment by incorporating into its general phrases the more specific guarantees contained in the first eight amendments included in the Bill of Rights. The Court has sought, in Justice Cardozo's words, for those principles "of justice so rooted in the traditions and conscience of our people as to be ranked as fundamental."[13] However, referring to other parts of the Constitution may not be sufficient when interpreting a phrase like "due process of law," which has a historical resonance recalling Runnymede and the Magna Carta.

As hard to interpret as the Fourteenth Amendment is, other parts of the Constitution have been deemed so obscure as to wholly defy judicial interpretation. Consider the Ninth Amendment: "The enumeration in the Constitution of certain rights shall not be construed to deny or disparage others retained by the people." Which other rights do citizens retain under the Constitution? The Ninth Amendment sets a moral question for constitutional interpreters: What rights do people "naturally" have and retain under the Constitution? It is disappointing, but perhaps not surprising, that Supreme Court justices and other constitutional interpreters have typically fled from the hard moral judgments called for by the Ninth Amendment.

How, then, are judges to decide what the Constitution requires in hard cases? They begin with the text itself and seek to understand not only the words but the structure of the document as a whole,

---

[13]*Palko* v. *Connecticut*, 302 U.S. 319 (1937).

the nature of the institutions it sets up, the powers and rights it enumerates, and the principles and purposes implicit in these words, structures, institutions, powers, and rights. Supreme Court justices also have to contend with a 200-year accumulation of thickly textured constitutional case law—interpretations that have helped give substance to the Constitution in previous cases, that have been relied on by lower-court judges, and that may have become part of the public's understanding of our fundamental law. Received authoritative interpretations and practices deserve to be taken seriously. And yet, the Constitution declares itself to be supreme and requires that judges take an oath to support the document itself, rather than past judicial interpretations of it. The Supreme Court, and any other constitutional interpreters, may decide that an established line of interpretation is mistaken.

While text, structure, implicit nature, principle, purpose, and precedent are always helpful guides in constitutional interpretation, they will not suffice for many tough issues. A justice might doubt, for instance, that the Ninth Amendment has been taken seriously enough; he might suspect that people have fundamental rights that are being ignored. But how does he decide what these rights are? Besides using text, structure, and precedent, a justice considering what rights Americans have may turn to our political traditions and to moral philosophy.

Partisans of the New Right seek to constrain the judicial search for constitutional meaning. They insist, as Richard Nixon once did, that Supreme Court justices should be "strict constructionists": they must be prepared to enforce the law as it is and not "twist or bend" it to suit their own personal political convictions.[14] As Bork puts it, "the judge must stick close to the text and the history."[15] These guidelines appear to be innocent enough, but appearances sometimes deceive. By admitting only those rights specifically envisioned by the Framers, the New Right hopes to straitjacket the Constitution's broad protections for liberty by precluding judicial reflection on the Constitution's more general moral purposes. By sticking to strict constructions and historical intentions, judges, say the conservatives, remain within their limited and precarious mandate to review legislative acts in light of the Constitution.

[14]Richard M. Nixon, as quoted in Ronald Dworkin, *Taking Rights Seriously* (Cambridge: Harvard University Press, 1977), p. 131.

[15]Bork, "Neutral Principles," p. 8.

The case for strict constructionism and historical intent is supported by particular notions of democratic authority and individual liberty that are considered later in this book. Here, it is worth considering in some detail the hurdles that must be cleared by the Jurisprudence of Original Intent—hurdles that are sidestepped by Bork and Meese.

First of all, whose intent is to count as original and authoritative? Who were "the Framers," and how are we to make sense of the idea that this large and disparate group had a unified "intent"? Should the intentions of all the delegates to the 1787 constitutional convention in Philadelphia be counted equally, or should the intentions of those who took a leading role in drafting the text count for more? Given the rather spotty records, one would need to rely on the intent of the leading advocates, but clearly, such individuals as Alexander Hamilton and James Madison were proponents of particular and, as it turned out later, different theories of the Constitution.

It was, of course, ratification that gave the Constitution the force of fundamental law, so why should the intentions of the Philadelphia delegates be counted but not the intentions of participants in the state ratifying conventions? Scholarly proponents of Original Intent, like Raoul Berger, seek the intentions of those in Congress who proposed the Fourteenth Amendment, rather than the more elusive but more pertinent intentions of those who secured its ratification in the states.[16]

Should the intentions of those who seem to have misunderstood what was being voted on be discounted? Perhaps, but no such judgment can be made without some independent conception of what the Constitution really means, and that is exactly what the conservatives think we do not and cannot have. In short, simply deciding whose intent counts proves to be quite difficult: it requires an elaborate theory and considerable historical research.

The second problem is to decide what counts as evidence of intent. William Crosskey undertook prodigious research in unpublished correspondence and manuscripts in his quest for the Framers'

---

[16]See Raoul Berger, *Government by Judiciary: The Transformation of the Fourteenth Amendment* (Cambridge: Harvard University Press, 1977).

intent.[17] Raoul Berger, on the other hand, considers only the public, published record of the passing of the Fourteenth Amendment, *The Congressional Globe*, in trying to determine the intent of the Framers of that crucial part of the Constitution. Yet, records of congressional proceedings may have been edited as is today's *Congressional Record*.

As for the Constitution itself, no official record of the closed proceedings in Philadelphia was ever published, an incomprehensible oversight if it had been expected that future interpreters would be guided by the Framers' intentions. The official record of the convention recorded motions and votes, but not speeches. James Madison's unofficial account of the convention, reconstructed from his notes, was published posthumously in 1840, after everyone who had attended the convention was dead.[18] Meese, however, in defending his Jurisprudence of Original Intent, claims, "The disputes and compromises of the Constitutional Convention were carefully recorded. The minutes of the Convention are a matter of public record."[19]

Even if we were to accept Madison's account of the convention as authoritative and complete, we would still need to confront the fact that public statements often do not reflect actual intentions. How would we distinguish between genuine evidence of intent and the delegates' posturings, rationalizations, and statements for public or scholarly or historical consumption? More basically, just what are intentions in this instance? Are they the Framers' expectations as to how particular provisions would be interpreted, or are they the Framers' hopes?[20] And what of the intentions of those legislators who did not speak?

Let us suppose that the first two hurdles have, against all odds, been cleared: we have decided whose intentions are to count and what is to count as evidence of intent. But after all this labor, we

[17]See William B. Crosskey, *Politics and the Constitution in the History of the United States*, 2 vols. (Chicago: Chicago University Press, Midway Reprint Series, 1978), vol. 1, pp. 3–14. Here, and in this section generally, the discussion draws upon the excellent Walter F. Murphy, "Constitutional Interpretation: The Art of the Historian, Magician, or Statesman?" *Yale Law Journal* 87 (1978), pp. 1752–71.

[18]See Winton U. Solberg, *The Federal Convention and the Formation of the Union of American States* (Indianapolis: Bobbs-Merrill Co., 1976), pp. 67–70.

[19]Meese, Federalist Society address, p. 2.

[20]See Ronald Dworkin's important discussion of the problems of Original Intent in "The Forum of Principle," *New York University Law Review* 56 (1981), reprinted in idem, *A Matter of Principle* (Cambridge: Harvard University Press, 1985).

find that the intentions of those involved in the long and arduous process of proposing and ratifying a constitutional amendment are complex and conflicting. We find that vague and general language cloaks disagreement and constitutes a delegation to future interpreters.

Conservative proponents of the Jurisprudence of Original Intent ignore the crucial distinction between language that is ambiguous, admitting of different but specific meanings, and language that is vague or general. As John Hart Ely argues, "The choice of a general term should, in the absence of contrary evidence, be assumed to have been conscious."[21] Indeed, Meese implies that we should accept the Constitution's general phrases as written and interpret them as such, but he fails to understand that in so doing he undermines his own reliance on specific historical intentions: "Those who framed the Constitution chose their words carefully; they debated at great length the most minute points. The language they chose meant something."[22] To rely on specific but unstated intentions is to ignore the obvious generality and sweep of the language actually chosen. The conservatives would substitute narrow, specific intentions for the broad terms that became fundamental law. The search for specific intentions represents not reverence for, but a misunderstanding of, the project of the Framers.

When it comes to defining constitutionally protected freedoms, conservatives claim that judges should protect only the specific sorts of activities the Framers had in mind. Judges are bound, say the conservatives, to enforce not their best understanding of the general concept chosen by the Framers, but only specific examples of the general concept that some Framers may have had in mind in circumstances very different from our own. However, the Framers of the Constitution were perfectly capable of being specific when they wanted to be: they said, for instance, that the president must "have attained the age of thirty five years," not "the President must be mature." And as Justice Frankfurter pointed out in *Adamson* v. *California*, what was voted on at each stage was the proposed language or amendment, not the speeches.[23] Surely there is no reason to suppose, as do the conservatives, that judges are obliged to read

[21]John Hart Ely, *Democracy and Distrust* (Cambridge: Harvard University Press, 1981), pp. 198–99.

[22]Meese, ABA address, p. 16.

[23]332 U.S. 46 (1947).

the Framers' sweeping phrases narrowly, in light of specific unstated intentions, given that the Framers could have used more specific phrases but chose not to.

The Fourteenth Amendment, for instance, requires that no state shall "deny to any person within its jurisdiction the equal protection of the laws." Should judges be confined to the specific kinds of unequal protection that the "framers" of that amendment might have had in mind? That is, if many of those responsible for the Fourteenth Amendment expected, foresaw, or hoped that it would prohibit racial discrimination in common law but not other forms of invidious discrimination, are judges bound by that concrete, unstated, "intention" to allow all other forms of discrimination, as Bork has claimed?[24] Judges could, instead, seek and apply the morally best understanding of the principles and values that give substance to the sweeping phrase "the equal protection of the laws." Judges seeking the morally best meaning would not engage in historical research designed to "resurrect" the intentions of persons long dead, as the New Right would have us do. Rather, they would seek the meaning that makes equal protection the most worthy value or goal consistent with the other values and goals in the Constitution.

There are many reasons for preferring the latter alternative. Constitutional principles must be applied to circumstances the Framers never envisioned. Even when institutions persist, the passage of time may alter their status in society; public schooling is a good example of that. Further, it may be that particular Framers, at the concrete level, inadequately understood what "the equal protection of the laws" actually requires. The supremacy of the Constitution as written, general sweeping phrases and all, may require specific judicial measures that the Framers of particular clauses did not contemplate.[25] Finally, the best reason for even acknowledging the supremacy of the Constitution is the document's conformity with our best understanding of justice. By engaging in moral reflection rather than historical research to complete the meaning of the Constitution's difficult passages, judges help justify and vindicate the

[24]Bork, "Neutral Principles," p. 14.

[25]See Dworkin's important claim that the Framers should be understood as having enacted general concepts into law, such as "equal protection," but not specific conceptions of what are to count as concrete instances of those concepts, in *Taking Rights Seriously*, pp. 134–36.

12

Constitution's moral supremacy, help to realize the Constitution's moral aspirations, and help to ensure that we will be governed by more than the will and preferences of the most powerful.

It is with good reason that constitutional scholar Walter F. Murphy argues, "The difficulties that confront any painstakingly thorough and intellectually scrupulous researcher who tries to establish legislative intent are typically insuperable."[26] At the very least, it would take an extremely elaborate theory, a series of difficult judgments, and a wealth of historical research to hack through the great tangle of problems surrounding the Jurisprudence of Original Intent. What began as a flight from hard judgments, therefore, ends in a series of nearly impossible judgments and insuperable obstacles.

The infirmities of the Jurisprudence of Original Intent appear to be fatal. Yet, there is one final disability that would alone prove fatal even to a theory healthy in other respects. Raoul Berger, whose *Government by Judiciary* indicts judicial activism in the name of Original Intent, asserts what other conservatives, like Bork, simply assume: that the Constitution "was written against a background of interpretive presuppositions" and, in particular, that the Framers intended future interpreters to carry out their "original" intentions.[27] If the conservatives are wrong about this particular intention, which we might call the original "interpretive intent," then the Jurisprudence of Original Intent self-destructs. If the Framers themselves did not intend constitutional interpreters to be guided by their specific intentions, then, if only to carry out the original intent, we would have to give up historical research and think about the Constitution for ourselves.

Unfortunately for the New Right, the Framers of the Constitution did reject reliance on historical intentions. The "modern resort to the 'intent of the framers' can gain no support from the assertion that such was the framers' expectation, for the framers themselves did not believe such an interpretive strategy to be appropriate," writes H. Jefferson Powell in his painstaking and impressive study of the historical record. He concludes that "there is no indication that they [the Philadelphia Framers] expected or intended future

[26]Murphy, p. 1761.

[27]Berger, pp. 365–66, quoted in H. Jefferson Powell, "The Original Understanding of Original Intent," *Harvard Law Review* 98 (1985): 886.

13

interpreters to resort to any extra-constitutional intentions revealed in the convention's secretly conducted debates."[28]

So how did the Founders expect the Constitution to be interpreted? There was no original consensus; rather, there were two different views on the subject. Many Americans of the revolutionary period, influenced by the Protestant idea that the truth of scripture or law resides in the common understanding of plain words, were suspicious of any sort of interpretation at all. Others embraced the rich interpretive tradition of the English common law, in which time-honored techniques for interpreting statutes, wills, and contracts were considered an authoritative part of the law itself.

Most of the Framers of the Constitution were, of course, lawyers. When faced with the task of interpreting ambiguous statutes, colonial lawyers and judges did not look to legislative history, as the modern proponents of Original Intent would have us do. Legal practice during that period specified that judges might look to an ambiguous act's preamble to determine its apparent end or purpose, as well as to its relation to previous acts and other legal precedents, but not to legislative history or to evidence of the subjective purposes of legislators.[29]

During the debates in the states over the ratification of the Constitution, the Framers had ample opportunity to affirm the controlling authority of their intentions, if they had so wished. But to the contrary, James Madison and Alexander Hamilton, who were most prominent in framing and securing the ratification of the Constitution, positively opposed reliance on the intentions of the Framers. They stressed that fallibility and tentativeness were inescapable features of human expression. Constitutional meaning would have to be elucidated and extended by judges in the course of adjudication through reasoned, legal deliberation, not by historical research. As Hamilton put it, "The rules of legal interpretation are rules of common sense, adopted by the courts in the construction of the laws. . . . In relation to such a subject [a constitution], the natural and obvious sense of its provisions, apart from any technical rules, is the true criterion of construction."[30]

Madison emphasized that the judiciary would play a necessary

[28]Powell, p. 903.
[29]Ibid., pp. 896–98.
[30]Alexander Hamilton, *Federalist*, no. 83.

14

part in fleshing out the meaning of the law of the land, which included the Constitution:

> All new laws, though penned with the greatest technical skill, and passed on the fullest and most mature deliberation, are considered as more or less obscure and equivocal, until their meaning be liquidated and ascertained by a series of particular discussions and adjudications.[31]

Some years after the ratification of the Constitution, when debating the constitutionality of the national bank bill, Hamilton explicitly rejected the relevance of historical evidence of the Framers' intentions:

> Whatever may have been the intention of the framers of a constitution, or of a law, that intention is to be sought for in the instrument itself, according to the usual and established rules of construction. Nothing is more common than for laws to express and effect, more or less than was intended.[32]

If the ideas of the Founders at the time they drafted and passed the Constitution positively oppose the Jurisprudence of Original Intent, some slightly later ideas seem, at first, more congenial to it.

The Republican theory of the Constitution, as developed and promoted by Thomas Jefferson and James Madison, secured national consensus 10 years into the life of the republic, a consensus that lasted for a quarter of a century.[33] The Republicans in the early 19th century, like Bork and the New Right generally today, were deeply suspicious of the "wiles of construction," or what they perceived as the tendency to distort the meaning of the Constitution in interpreting it. Like Bork, the Republicans saw constitutional interpretation as a search for the Constitution's underlying and original intent.[34] On its surface, therefore, the Republican theory of the Constitution seems to be a precursor of the Jurisprudence of Original Intent.

But modern conservative intentionalism is not supported by the

---

[31]James Madison, *Federalist*, no. 37.

[32]Alexander Hamilton, "Opinion on the Constitutionality of an Act to Establish a Bank" (1791), reprinted in *Eight Papers of Alexander Hamilton*, ed. H. Syrett (1965), p. 111, quoted in Powell, p. 915.

[33]Powell, p. 887.

[34]Ibid., p. 927.

Republican theory of the Constitution. Republican strict constructionism derived from an understanding of the Constitution as a compact between the states, which retained their sovereignty. Strict constructionism was justified, for the Republicans, by their conviction that sovereign states could not be presumed to have given up more of their powers than they explicitly specified in the Constitution. Thus, the Republicans were mainly concerned about interpreting the federal government's powers narrowly. In contrast, Bork seeks to read federal powers broadly and to read reservations on those powers, including individual rights, narrowly.

Indeed, the Republican theory of the Constitution was developed in direct opposition to nationalists, like Hamilton, who interpreted federal powers broadly. According to the Republican-inspired Virginia and Kentucky Resolutions of 1798 drafted by Madison and Jefferson, the states retained the right to review federal interpretations of the Constitution and to reject those they disagreed with.

Republican strict constructionism depended basically on the assumption that the states retained their sovereignty as parties to a constitutional compact. Bork's argument for strict construction, however, rests on the wholly different assumption that the Constitution gains its authority from the will of a sovereign national majority, which cannot be supposed to have ceded more rights to minorities than were expressly granted. Nothing could be further from the minds of Jefferson and Madison than Bork's claim that the Constitution establishes a national democracy of broad powers with few reservations on these powers. The legal positivism that undergirds Bork's position, the idea that the Constitution is authoritative because of its source in popular will, is deeply at odds with the founding generation's belief that principles of justice and natural rights are morally binding on any act of will. The strict constructionism of Bork and other present-day conservatives is clearly at odds with the ideas of the Founding Fathers.

Some conservatives do argue for a return to the old Republican "states' rights" conception of the Constitution. In fact, many conservatives make more of federalism than does Robert Bork. Meese, for example, approvingly cites Justice Rehnquist's opinion in *National League of Cities* v. *Usery*,[35] in which Rehnquist flirts with the states'-rights view by speaking of "the states in their capacities as sovereign governments" and refers to states as "coordinate elements in the

[35]426 U.S. 833 (1976).

16

system established by the framers."[36] Other conservatives contend, more reasonably, that the federal government has assumed powers that properly belong to the states, especially certain "police powers," powers to regulate health and safety, powers not related to commerce and national defense, and powers not grounded by any reasonable construction in the Constitution's enumeration of Congress's powers.[37]

It is one thing to argue that the federal government has assumed powers reserved to the states, making a mockery of both federalism and a government of enumerated powers. It is quite another thing, and far more difficult, to maintain that the federal government has overstepped its bounds in defending constitutional rights against the states. The scope of legitimate national powers may be more limited than the powers actually accrued by the federal government, but nothing follows from this claim as to the propriety of the Supreme Court's protection of a broad sphere of national rights. The Thirteenth, Fourteenth, and Fifteenth amendments—adopted after the Civil War—decisively shift to the national government the responsibility for protecting a broad sphere of individual rights against the states.

The old Republican theory, which depicts the Constitution as a compact among sovereign states, and the modern conservative idea, which depicts America as essentially a majoritarian democracy, have one important attribute in common: both are based on implausible conceptions of the fundamental nature of the republic. The Republican claim that the Constitution is basically a compact among the states is undermined by the fact that the Constitution emanates from and operates directly on the people of the whole nation. "We, the people of the United States," as the preamble indicates, and not the states, ordained and established the Constitution as fundamental law.

Proponents of the modern Jurisprudence of Original Intent, on the other hand, ignore the fact that the Constitution established, and was meant to establish, not a majoritarian democracy but a liberal, or constitutional, democracy. The legitimacy of the national

[36]Meese, AEI address, p. 3; idem, ABA address, pp. 6–7.

[37]See chapter 3 below. See also Sotirios Barber's important claim that congressional powers have been used pretextually as a substitute for an adequate theory of constitutional ends, given in idem, *On What the Constitution Means* (Baltimore: Johns Hopkins Press, 1984), especially pp. 101–6.

government does rest on the consent of the governed, but not on that alone. Although our scheme of government utilizes some forms of democratic accountability, it remains a system of enumerated or limited powers and broad rights. In short, the Constitution expresses a certain measure of confidence in, but also no small measure of distrust of, democratic government. For the people who drafted and ratified the Constitution, legitimate government depended not only on the document's origin in popular consent, but also on its conformity with certain principles of justice and "unalienable Rights," which were held to be "natural" or of higher moral standing than the will of any majority.

The modern Jurisprudence of Original Intent, therefore, cannot gain support from what is only a superficial similarity to the old Republican theory of the Constitution. Consequently, there is no reason to think that the Founders intended future interpreters to be guided by the Founders' own specific intentions rather than by the general purposes set out in the Constitution itself. The Constitution declares itself to be supreme, and the preamble lays out its objects and purposes in broad terms, including "Justice" and "the Blessings of Liberty for ourselves and our Posterity." The very language of the Constitution suggests that the Framers, as intelligent statesmen, recognized that the Constitution is not a contract or a statute but a majestic charter for government, intended to govern for ages to come and to apply to both unforeseen and unforeseeable circumstances. The notion that specific but unstated intentions ought to supplant the interpreter's best understanding of the general words and structure of the document represents a devaluation of the status of the document itself. It is in light of the aspiration to justice and liberty, and the other objects and ends stated and implied in the Constitution, that the founding document and its problematic passages should be interpreted. By misunderstanding the purpose of the generation that resorted to constitutionalism, the proponents of the Jurisprudence of Original Intent have planted the seeds of their own destruction.

What accounts for the allure of the Jurisprudence of Original Intent? What has led the New Right to adopt a position so fraught with difficulties and so patently at odds with the spirit of the Constitution? For judges seeking to avoid making difficult judgments of political morality, resort to the Framers' intentions appears, at first, to be an avenue of escape. And for those seeking to constrain the discretion and political influence of judges, Original Intent appears to be a useful straitjacket. Original Intent, however, can be neither an escape nor a straitjacket, for there is no simple canonical intent locked in the historical record waiting to be uncovered and deferred to. Nor can conscientious interpreters avoid making difficult judgments, for the Constitution itself will not allow it. Judges who wish to live up to their oath to support the Constitution cannot avoid the difficult political judgments with which the founding document confronts them. And those who invoke, against a robust judiciary, the founding document and the intent of its Framers have understood neither.

In any case, the conservative invocation of Original Intent has less to do with reverence for the ideas of the Founders than with a political preference for majoritarian power over individual rights and liberty. The Jurisprudence of Original Intent would render constitutionalism a mere mask, concealing without directing or constraining the sovereign power of majorities. Underlying Bork's version of the Constitution is a majoritarian impulse that, far from being in accord with the intentions of the Framers, is deeply at odds both with the text and structure of the Constitution and the project of constitutionalism itself.

III. The Majoritarian Myth

Despite the great popularity of the argument for Original Intent, it is a singularly problematic and unpromising way to interpret the Constitution. The real basis of the New Right's jurisprudence is not reverence for historical or original intentions anyway, as is evident from the fact that the conservatives are selective rather than consistent in their invocation of Original Intent. If the conservatives were really interested in honoring historical intentions, they would not simply assert, with Bork, that "the framers' intentions with respect to freedoms are the sole legitimate premise" for "constitutional analysis."[38] Rather, consistent and conscientious proponents of Original Intent would interpret not only freedoms in light of specific intentions but also government powers.

What the New Right position really comes down to is the Jurisprudence of Selective Intent: judges are referred to original intentions only when the process serves a deeper political commitment—that of construing government powers and the powers of majorities broadly and individual rights narrowly. This preference for political power over individual rights controls the conservatives' use of the idea of Original Intent and thereby forms the real basis of their theory of the Constitution. In fact, the New Right's commitment to majoritarianism and government power is deeply opposed to the only intentions that really count, namely, those embodied by the Framers in the text of the Constitution.

Innumerable analyses of the Constitution begin with the assumption that America is basically a democratic polity. As Alexander Bickel put it, "Judicial review is a deviant institution in the American democracy."[39] Judges are unelected and are responsible to no constituency, and their power is most controversial when the courts review the acts of elected legislators for conformity with the Constitution. Given the assumption that America is basically a majori-

---

[38]Bork, *Tradition*, p. 10.

[39]Alexander Bickel, *The Least Dangerous Branch* (Indianapolis: Bobbs-Merrill Co., 1962), p. 18.

tarian democratic polity, judicial review stands out as an anomaly, and the imposition of limits on the review power of judges appears as an imperative. And so Judge Antonin Scalia, another Reagan appointee often mentioned as a potential Supreme Court nominee, advocates a "restricted view of the Court's role in a democratic society."[40]

The New Right's majoritarian convictions are straightforward, though sometimes couched in the language of liberty. Thus, Bork quotes the English writer G. K. Chesterton:

> "What is the good of telling a community that it has every liberty except the liberty to make laws? The liberty to make laws is what constitutes a free people." The makers of our Constitution thought so too, for they provided wide powers to representative assemblies and ruled only a few subjects off limits by the Constitution.[41]

Bork depicts judicial deference to legislatures as an avoidance of value choice:

> The choice of "fundamental values" by the Court cannot be justified. Where constitutional materials do not clearly specify the value to be preferred, there is no principled way to prefer any claimed human value to any other. The judge must stick close to the text and history, and their fair implications, and not construct any new rights.[42]

Judicial deference, however, is not an avoidance of choice. Rather, it is a choice of majority power over individual liberty. This choice of political values is as "fundamental" and important as any choice can be, and it needs to be defended or abandoned, not hidden under the guise of skepticism, deference, and neutrality.

The selective invocation of Original Intent hides a decided political bias:

> A position that upholds constitutional claims only if they were within the specific contemplation of the Framers in effect establishes a presumption of resolving textual ambiguities against the

---

[40]Antonin Scalia, "Economic Affairs as Human Affairs," *Cato Journal* 4, no. 3 (1985): 707.

[41]Bork, *Tradition*, p. 9.

[42]Bork, "Neutral Principles," p. 8. On Bork's opposition to the "method of moral philosophy," see also idem, "Commentary: The Impossibility of Finding Welfare Rights in the Constitution," *Washington University Law Quarterly* (1979): 695–97.

claims of constitutional right. This is a choice no less political than any other; it expresses antipathy to the claims of the minority against the majority.[43]

Conservative strict constructionists, like Bork, argue in effect that judges should enforce only explicit rights, rights plainly stated in the Constitution's text or very clearly implied in it. Legislators, on the other hand, may do anything that is not plainly forbidden by the Constitution's text and its clear implications. This stark divergence of standards can be justified only by a strong assumption that the overall purpose or point of the Constitution is to empower majoritarian institutions.

The democratic rendering of the Constitution is a crucial underpinning of the selective invocation of Original Intent and of the New Right's attack on the judiciary. But the New Right's strategy for defining individual rights narrowly and government powers broadly rests on a nonexistent foundation: the Constitution is not basically a simple democratic document.

The Philadelphia constitutional convention took place under the shadow of chaos and instability in the states, which the Framers attributed to excessive democracy in the state constitutions under the Articles of Confederation.[44] In the eleven years between the signing of the Declaration of Independence and the Philadelphia convention, those who would frame the Constitution learned that making government accountable to the people is not sufficient to secure either order or the protection of liberty and rights.

Direct democracy and majoritarianism were decisively rejected by the Framers, and the system of government established by the Constitution embodies this rejection.[45] Senators were originally chosen by state legislators, and it was only in 1913, with the passage of the Seventeenth Amendment, that they became popularly elected; even so, each state continues to have two senators regardless of population. State legislatures were originally given the power to choose presidential electors, and the less-populous states continue to be overrepresented in the electoral college. Staggered elections,

---

[43]William J. Brennan, speech at Georgetown University, October 12, 1985; reprinted in New York Times, October 13, 1985, p. 36. Brennan's own reading of the Constitution is, however, no less partisan and selective than that of the New Right.

[44]See Gordon Wood, The Creation of the American Republic: 1776–1787 (New York: W. W. Norton & Company, 1969).

[45]See the Federalist, especially no. 10 and no. 49.

long terms for senators and the president, the system of separated powers, and the embrace by one national government of a large or "extended" republic were all designed by the Framers to make it difficult for a national majority to gain effective control of the government. It was thereby hoped that ample room would be left for deliberation, statesmanship, and the rule of justice. On the "input" or process side, therefore, democracy is tempered and compromised by many checks and balances, including the power of the courts.

As for the courts, it is sometimes argued that those who have libertarian political sentiments should press these sentiments in the political arena along with everyone else. For proponents of rights who lose in the political process to then invoke the power of courts is as illegitimate, as Bork puts it, as invoking the power of the joint chiefs of staff; in either case, it amounts to the perpetration of "limited coups d'etat."[46] The courts have a narrow role, limited to enforcing the specific prohibitions of the Constitution along the lines suggested by the concrete historical intentions of the Founders. Here again, these prescriptions are supported by the implicit idea that the Court's power is somehow anomalous or in need of being circumscribed in a democratic polity.

Nevertheless, it is hard to find any warrant for this presumption against the courts in the Constitution itself. The founding document extends the judicial power "to all Cases, in Law and Equity, arising under this Constitution."[47] Judges take an oath to support the Constitution, and in declaring itself supreme, the Constitution then adds that judges should take special notice: "This Constitution, and the Laws of the United States which shall be made in pursuance thereof . . . shall be the supreme Law of the Land; and the judges in every State shall be bound thereby."[48]

In the first Congress, James Madison proposed and led the passage of the Bill of Rights, explaining that once passed and "incorporated into the Constitution, independent tribunals of justice will consider themselves in a peculiar manner the guardians of those rights." The courts, Madison continued, will be an "impenetrable bulwark against every assumption of power in the legislative or executive" branches and "be naturally led to resist every encroach-

[46]Bork, "Neutral Principles," p. 6.
[47]U.S. Constitution, Article III, sec. 2.
[48]Ibid., Article VI.

24

ment upon rights expressly stipulated for in the Constitution by the declaration of rights."[49]

The *Federalist*, no. 78, was Hamilton's extended defense of an independent, active judiciary. He defined limited government as one that protects individual rights through the courts even against "legislative invasions . . . instigated by the major voice of the community." Those who doubt that the Framers intended the judiciary to play an active role in preserving limited government and individual rights even against popular majorities should pay heed to Hamilton's public declaration:

> The courts were designed to be an intermediate body between the people and the legislature in order, among other things, to keep the latter within the limits of their assigned authority. The interpretation of the laws is the proper and peculiar province of the courts. A constitution is, in fact, and must be regarded by judges as, a fundamental law. . . . [T]he constitution ought to be preferred to the statute. . . . This independence of judges is equally requisite to guard the constitution and rights of individuals from the effects of those ill humors which the arts of designing men, or the influence of particular conjunctures, sometimes disseminate among the people themselves . . . to occasion dangerous innovations in the government, and serious oppressions of the minor party in the community. . . . [I]t would require an uncommon portion of fortitude in the judges to do their duty as faithful guardians of the Constitution, where legislative invasions of it had been instigated by the major voice of the community.[50]

Thus, Hamilton defended the "permanent tenure of judicial offices" so as to make the courts "bulwarks of a limited constitution against legislative encroachments."

The Framers of the Constitution, therefore, took pains to check popular will and not simply to empower it because they agreed with Madison that "the invasion of private rights is chiefly to be apprehended, not from acts of Government contrary to the sense

---

[49]James Madison, as quoted in Robert Rutland, "How the Constitution Secures Rights: A Look at the Seminal Years," in *How Does the Constitution Secure Rights?* ed. Robert Goldwin and William Schambra (Washington: American Enterprise Institute, 1985).

[50]Alexander Hamilton, *Federalist*, no. 78.

of its constituents, but from acts in which the Government is the mere instrument of the major number of constituents."[51]

So much for the claim that the Constitution establishes simple, democratic processes. The Constitution also imposes a number of substantive limitations on the ends the federal government may pursue. The Constitution explicitly denies Congress the power to suspend habeas corpus in peacetime, to pass bills of attainder, to pass ex post facto laws, or undertake certain other actions.[52] It also explicitly denies to the states the power to conduct their own foreign policies, grant titles of nobility, emit bills of credit, make paper money legal tender, pass bills of attainder and ex post facto laws, or impair the obligation of contracts.[53]

The Constitution's specific prohibitions may seem rather thin; indeed, one of the chief complaints of those who opposed ratification of the Constitution was the absence of a bill of rights limiting the power of the national government in the name of fundamental rights and liberties. This absence, however, was not the consequence of any skepticism on the part of the Framers about the existence of broad natural rights. There was probably nothing in politics that the founding generation was more certain of than the existence of natural rights.

As Hamilton explained in the *Federalist*, the enumeration of rights in a Constitution could, paradoxically, be harmful to rights themselves. The Founders distrusted the "aphorisms" that tended to be embodied in bills of rights. More importantly, they positively opposed the natural implication of an enumeration of rights; to specify the rights to be protected against oppressive majorities might imply, wrongly, that these rights were exceptions to a general grant of government powers.[54]

A government of enumerated powers need not specify the rights to be protected against the power of majorities. "The Constitution is itself," as Hamilton put it in the *Federalist*, no. 84, "in every rational sense, and to every useful purpose, A BILL OF RIGHTS."

[51]James Madison, letter to Thomas Jefferson (1788), quoted in Walter Murphy, "The Art of Constitutional Interpretation," in *Essays on the Constitution of the United States*, ed. M. Judd Harmon (Port Washington, N.Y.: Kennikat, 1978), pp. 130–59.

[52]See U.S. Constitution, Article I, sec. 9.

[53]Ibid.

[54]Alexander Hamilton, *Federalist*, no. 84. See the discussion in Herbert Storing, "The Constitution and the Bill of Rights," in Harmon, *Essays*, pp. 32–48.

When conservatives like Bork treat rights as islands surrounded by a sea of government powers, they precisely reverse the view of the Founders as enshrined in the Constitution, wherein government powers are limited and specified and rendered as islands surrounded by a sea of individual rights.

To help quiet the fears of the Anti-Federalists, the proponents of the Constitution did eventually propose a Bill of Rights in the first Congress. But the logic of limited government was not overturned. Madison imbedded this logic in the Bill of Rights itself. Thus, to the first eight amendments, which specify various liberties to be protected against government, were added the Ninth Amendment, which explicitly denies that popular rights could be limited to those enumerated in the Constitution, and the Tenth Amendment, which reserves all powers not delegated to the federal government to the states and the people.

Given that the Founders originally believed that the need for a Bill of Rights had been preempted by the limited nature of national government powers, constitutional interpreters should not be so preoccupied with the Bill of Rights as to neglect the power-limiting logic of the Constitution itself. Whereas the president is granted "The Executive Power," and the courts "The Judicial Power," Congress is conspicuously given only "all legislative powers *herein granted*" (emphasis added). Legislative powers are specifically enumerated and not general.

Just how narrowly the specific grants of legislative powers should be read is a hard question of constitutional interpretation, a harder question than the conservatives admit. Article I, section 8, of the Constitution enumerates Congress's powers. The first eight powers concern commerce broadly: the powers to tax, to borrow money on credit, to regulate commerce, to establish uniform rules for naturalization and bankruptcy, to "coin money," to punish counterfeiting, to establish post offices, and to grant exclusive patents and copyrights. The other powers granted to Congress provide for the establishment of lower courts, for the governing of the District of Columbia, and, most importantly, for national security. At the end of section 8 stands the "necessary and proper" clause: Congress may "make all laws which shall be necessary and proper for carrying into Execution the foregoing Powers, and all other Powers vested by this Constitution in the Government of the United States."

The "necessary and proper" clause certainly allows Congress to do many things incidentally required to carry out the enumerated powers. In the early years of the republic, however, a much broader way of reading the seemingly narrow grants of legislative power was devised by Chief Justice Marshall.

The case of *McCulloch* v. *Maryland* raised the question of the constitutionality of a bill establishing a national bank.[55] Nowhere does the Constitution specifically give this power to Congress, and Thomas Jefferson, among others, argued that the establishment of a bank was beyond the powers of the national government.

Marshall's decision in *McCulloch*, one of the most important ever handed down, was based on the claim that the specific grants of legislative power in Article I, section 8, are the "great outlines" of Congress's power. But the specific enumerations do not exhaust the means by which Congress may pursue its great ends. The very "nature" of a Constitution, said Marshall, requires that it avoid "the prolixity of a legal code," its "great outlines should be marked, its important objects designated, and the main ingredients which compose those objects deduced from the nature of the objects themselves." Although the Constitution does not specifically grant the power to establish a national bank, this power is, said Marshall, a legitimate means that facilitates the achievement of ends that are granted: to lay and collect taxes, to coin money, to regulate commerce, and to support armies and navies.

The logic of Marshall's argument is almost universally accepted today. At the time, however, it was rejected by such notables as Madison and Jefferson. They argued that Marshall's logic permitted Congress "to take possession of a boundless field of power, no longer susceptible of any definition," making a mockery of the idea of limited government.[56] This is not quite true. Even on Marshall's expansive reading, the great ends of the national government remain limited; Congress may not use its powers as "pretexts" to pursue ends not related to the promotion of commerce and national security.[57]

Despite its nearly universal acceptance, Marshall's logic is not unassailable. It is not true, for instance, that the Constitution's language on Congress's powers speaks only in "great outlines" and does "not enumerate means." Consider the following clause in

[55]4 Wheaton 316 (1819).

[56]Thomas Jefferson, as quoted in Gerald Gunther, *Cases and Materials on Constitutional Law* (Mineola, N.Y.: Foundation Press, 1980), p. 95.

[57]See Barber, chap. 4.

28

Article I, section 8: Congress may "promote the Progress of Science and useful Arts, by securing for limited Times to Authors and Inventors the exclusive Right to their respective Writings and Discoveries." This clause specifies both the end and the means, and it does so rather specifically. Even when read in light of the "necessary and proper" clause, it clearly implies that Congress may not promote "the Progress of Science and useful Arts" by means other than those specified. The part of the clause following the word "by" specifies how Congress may promote science and the arts, and it would be useless and inexplicable if Congress were free to choose any convenient means to that end. Thus, it is hard to see how one could establish the constitutionality of, say, the National Science Foundation.

Marshall's claim that the enumeration of powers in Article I, section 8, speaks only in "great outlines" or of vast powers is also untrue. Powers are listed that could have been derived by extrapolations less significant than that supporting the power to establish a national bank. After providing that an army and navy can be raised and supported, for instance, section 8 provides the power "to make Rules for the government and regulation of the land and naval forces."

There is certainly much more to be said on both sides of this important issue. Short shrift has been given here to Marshall's complex argument, to the arguments in the *Federalist* that might support his position, and to the formidable scholarly works that have defended his position. The purpose of this discussion is certainly not to prove that *McCulloch* was wrongly decided. Rather, it is, first, to make clear that Marshall's reasoning about Congress's powers, upon which a vast edifice of constitutional law has been erected, does not depend on any cramped literalism or on a search for an original intention. (If judges stuck "close to the text and its clear implications" when interpreting powers, as Bork says they should when interpreting rights, the national government would be very severely constrained indeed.)

A second purpose here is to make clear that, contrary to the claim of such conservatives as Bork, the Constitution does not establish a basically majoritarian democracy of broad powers and few minority rights. On its face, the Constitution's language with regard to powers is restrictive, and even on Marshall's expansive reading, national powers remain limited. Marshall's reasoning in *McCulloch* stretches, but does not fundamentally overturn, the logic of enumerated powers and limited legislative ends. And what we need to do next is note the expansive language of those provisions protecting individual liberties in the Bill of Rights.

The Constitution lends explicit support to the values of economic freedom, private security, property rights, and liberty of contract. Article I, section 10, prohibits any state "Law impairing the Obligation of Contracts." The Third Amendment protects the sanctity of the home against the quartering of troops, and the Fourth Amendment protects "The right of the people to be secure in their persons, houses, papers, and effects, against unreasonable searches and seizures." Personal security and privacy are thus clearly linked with property ownership. The Fifth Amendment brings life, liberty, and property under the protection of "due process of law," and this guarantee is explicitly extended to the states by the Fourteenth Amendment. The Fifth Amendment also requires that private property may be taken only for public use and with "just compensation."

There is, of course, considerable textual support in the Constitution for other, noneconomic liberties, including religious freedom and freedom of speech, of the press, and of assembly. The founding document also protects the many privileges and immunities associated with the rule of law and with fair proceedings in criminal cases, in the Fifth, Sixth, Seventh, and Eighth amendments. The Ninth Amendment, as noted, explicitly warns against construing the "enumeration" of "certain rights" to "deny or disparage others retained by the people." And the Tenth Amendment emphasizes that the powers of the federal government are limited to those "delegated" to it (though, of course, not necessarily to those expressly or explicitly enumerated). The Bill of Rights closes with the reminder that powers not delegated are "reserved to the States respectively, or to the people."

The Constitution is basically concerned not simply with empowering the people's representatives to govern, but with checking and limiting the powers of legislative majorities in a host of important ways, both procedurally and substantively (or on both the "input" and the "output" sides). The New Right's preoccupation with the legitimacy of judicial review ignores the fact that in a system of limited government, the exercise of legislative power itself demands positive constitutional support. Legislators and executives are bound, no less than judges are, to carry out their constitutional mandate. All who take an oath to support the Constitution as supreme law have an obligation to conscientiously strive toward its ends and purposes and not just to avoid breaking its most obvious commands. There is no presumption in the Constitution in favor of legislatures and against judges, or in favor of majority power and against individual rights and liberties. Judicial review is not an anomalous blotch on a democratic scheme of government. Contrary to what the conservatives hold, judicial review is an integral part of a scheme of constitutionally limited government.

How best to reconcile the logic of *McCulloch* with the Constitution's commitment to a broad expanse of individual rights is a hard question to be confronted by judges in adjudicating cases, and also by legislators and others when serving as conscientious interpreters. If one accepts the power-expanding logic of *McCulloch* and yet also construes rights expansively (as commanded by the Ninth Amendment), one has to undertake the hard, but far from impossible, task of drawing lines between the powers of the national government and the rights of individuals, and between the powers of the national government and the reserved powers of the states. What must be utterly unacceptable, to any conscientious interpreter, is a jurisprudence that ignores broad individual rights so well anchored in the Constitution.

IV. Morality and Constitutional Law

Before considering what, in substance, a principled constitutional jurisprudence should be, it is necessary to contend with the New Right's skeptical, derisive attitude toward the judicial invocation of moral principles. The New Right's moral skepticism is utterly implausible, ignoble, and deeply at odds with America's morally robust constitutional tradition.

Bork insists, uncontroversially, that judicial decisions must rest on "reasoned opinions," that is, a "legitimate" court must have "a valid theory, derived from the Constitution" to justify its actions.[58] Bork's view of what constitutes a constitutional principle is, however, extremely narrow: valid constitutional principles are drawn only from the text interpreted in light of specific historical intentions; the "framers' intentions with respect to freedoms are the sole legitimate premise from which constitutional analysis may proceed."[59] On Bork's reading, therefore, the equal protection clause of the Fourteenth Amendment has two requirements: "formal procedural equality," as the bare text clearly requires, and no government discrimination along racial lines, because a concern with race is revealed by the history of the Fourteenth Amendment.

Cut loose from plain text and historical intentions, there is, for Bork, "no principled way of saying which . . . inequalities are permissible."[60] Beyond text and historical intention are "matters of morality," which "belong . . . to the political community."[61] Political morality is of no help in deciding constitutional questions because, says Bork, any system of "moral and ethical values . . . has no objective or intrinsic validity of its own"; there is, in effect, no right and wrong because all that can be said about morality is that "men can and do differ."[62] As if to make moral skepticism or subjectivism

[58]Bork, "Neutral Principles," p. 3.
[59]Bork, *Tradition*, p. 10.
[60]Bork, "Neutral Principles," p. 11.
[61]Ibid., p. 12.
[62]Ibid., p. 10.

official U.S. government policy, Attorney General Meese approvingly quotes Bork's aphorism: "The judge who looks outside the Constitution always looks inside himself and nowhere else."[63]

Bork's skepticism turns to cynicism when he reduces all moral claims to claims for "gratification": "Every clash between a minority claiming freedom and a majority claiming power to regulate involves a choice between the gratifications of two groups."[64] When examining *Griswold* v. *Connecticut*, a case in which married couples asserted, as a matter of constitutional and political morality, the right to use contraceptives in the privacy of their own home, Bork sees no serious moral problem but only a question of "sexual gratification." Since there is no principled way, according to Bork, to discriminate between kinds of "gratification," the majority should have its way.[65] Bork would extend First Amendment protections only to *political* speech that is within the bounds of the established legal order; he would extend no judicial protection to academic, literary, or any other forms of expression.[66]

Justice Rehnquist, generally considered the intellectual leader of the conservative bloc on the Supreme Court, shares Bork's moral skepticism: "Many of us necessarily feel strongly and deeply about our own moral judgments, but they remain only personal moral judgments until in some way given the sanction of law."[67] What Rehnquist, like Bork, gives us is moral skepticism in the service of majoritarianism, masquerading as an innocent respect for the constitutional text.

Judge Posner expresses a similar skepticism about "value judgments":

> [It is] inevitable that many judicial decisions will be based on value judgments rather than technical determinations; and decisions so made are by definition not scientific, and therefore are not readily falsifiable and hence not readily verifiable either—and as a consequence are not always profitably discussable.[68]

[63]Meese, Federalist Society address, p. 11.

[64]Bork, "Neutral Principles," p. 9.

[65]Ibid., p. 11; and see *Griswold* v. *Connecticut*, 381 U.S. 479 (1965).

[66]Bork, "Neutral Principles," p. 20.

[67]William H. Rehnquist, "The Notion of a Living Constitution," *Texas Law Review* 54 (1976): 704.

[68]Richard A. Posner, "The Meaning of Judicial Self-Restraint," *Indiana Law Journal* 59 (1983): 6.

Although Posner's skepticism has a scientific gloss, and his position is arguably more sophisticated than Bork's, he agrees with Bork in urging judges to confine themselves to principles that have "public approbation" and "values that are widely . . . held" in the community.[69]

The New Right's attitude to rights claims appears to have the advantage of a tough-minded, down-to-earth, realism. Bork makes much of preferring the "common sense of the people" to the "theorists of moral abstraction," to "intellectuals," and to "what-have-you philosophy."[70] But the appearance of realism is spurious, for Americans could not make sense of their traditions, practices, and habitual ways of thinking, acting, and judging, or of the Constitution, if they accepted the New Right's radical moral skepticism. Indeed, it is hard to see how one could reconcile the New Right's apparently principled preference for democracy with its moral skepticism. (After all, why should anyone, except on the basis of a principle of moral equality, prefer the gratifications of the majority to a minority? Why should we prefer democracy to totalitarianism?)

The apparent lesson of the New Right's derision of rights and moral reflection is that moral claims can be ignored because they are no more than the way that "intellectuals" dress up their preferences and gratifications. In reducing rights claims to demands for "gratification," the New Right theorists destroy the distinction between moral reasons and mere arbitrary preferences. And as Sotirios Barber points out, to insist that a community's enforced ethical values need express no more than the merely subjective preferences of the majority is to put forward "a sophisticated version of the maxim that might makes right."[71]

In telling the majority, those with the strength of numbers, that morality may be ignored (because moral reasons are mere preferences), the New Right calls upon what is worst, not what is best, in the public. The Framers recognized this stance; indeed, they feared it. They feared the untutored, unrefined "prejudices" of the

[69]Ibid., pp. 10, 23.

[70]Bork, *Tradition*, pp. 7–11.

[71]Sotirios Barber, "Judge Bork's Constitution," in *Courts, Judges, and Politics*, 3d ed., ed. Walter F. Murphy and C. Herman Pritchett (New York: Random House, forthcoming), pp. 691–95. Barber also has pointed out to the present author that Bork's position is essentially the same as that of Thrasymachus, in Plato's *Republic*, who argued against Socrates that justice is no more than the interest of the stronger.

people, and they regarded those who would flatter and enflame these prejudices as demagogues.

The Framers feared the "passions" of the people, and they argued that "the reason, alone, of the public . . . ought to control and regulate the government."[72] The Framers were not simple democrats, but republicans who rejected the idea that popular government was necessarily good government. They sought to ensure that political power would be in the hands of the wisest members of the community and not those most responsive to popular prejudices: "The republican principle demands that the deliberate sense of the community should govern."[73] And, unlike Bork and others in today's New Right, the Framers were neither morally skeptical nor derisive of abstract ideas. For what else but abstract ideas are the "self-evident" truths of the Declaration of Independence? What else but philosophical principles are "unalienable Rights" that belong naturally to all men? And how else, except as the assertion of an abstract moral claim, can one understand the Framers' assertion that "Justice is the end of government"?[74]

Fortunately, despite its apparent tough-mindedness, the New Right's conception of morality is so counterintuitive that hardly anyone would accept it and so implausible that no one should. Who really believes that moral claims express only desires for "gratification," as Bork asserts? To accept Bork's position, one would have to believe that there is no moral difference between the "gratification" of a murderer and the "gratification" of his potential victim who wishes to live. According to Bork, "Anything some people want has, to that degree, social value."[75] But what of the desires of the rapist, the thief, and the arsonist? Do these desires have social value? And do they fail to win moral approval and become lawful only because they are the desires of minorities?

Contrary to Bork, the truth is that we can and do distinguish between mere gratifications and genuine moral claims all the time. We say with moral confidence that the gratifications of those who enjoy murdering, raping, stealing, burning other people's homes, or violating rights in other ways count for nothing. We believe in fundamental rights, to freedom of conscience and of speech, to life

[72]*Federalist*, no. 49.
[73]*Federalist*, no. 71.
[74]*Federalist*, no. 51.
[75]Bork, "Neutral Principles," p. 29.

and to at least some forms of privacy, on the basis of moral reason and not on the basis of absurd calculations about net gratifications.

The New Right's moral theory is nothing if not audacious, but it would take more than audacity to seriously argue either that the Framers of the Constitution shared this deep skepticism or that the American people do so today. The Framers were suspicious of democracy and confident that certain standards of political morality transcend the will of any majority. And they sought, in the deliberations on the ratification of the Constitution, to direct the public's attention toward reflection on justice and away from arbitrary preferences and immediate "gratifications": the conduct of this country would decide, said Hamilton in the first paragraph of the first *Federalist*, "whether societies of men are capable or not of establishing good government from reflection and choice" rather than "accident and force." And Thomas Paine expressed the faith of his generation when he claimed, "The Independence of America was accompanied by a Revolution in the principles and practices of Governments. . . . Government founded on a moral theory . . . on the indefeasible hereditary Rights of Man, is now revolving from West to East."[76]

Bork basks in his derision of moral abstractions and claims that his posture expresses reverence for the founders and our political tradition. But moral abstractions, such as rights and justice, did play a central role in the minds of the Founders and do form an essential part of America's constitutional tradition.

The main sources of the political ideas of the founding generation were the legal authorities Edward Coke and William Blackstone and the great classical liberal political theorist John Locke.[77] All three accepted the political centrality of "natural law" morality. Coke and Locke, in particular, continually stressed that moral standards

---

[76]Thomas Paine, *The Rights of Man*, quoted in Thomas Pangle, "Patriotism American Style," *National Review*, November 29, 1985, pp. 30–34.

[77]On the influence of Locke, see Bernard Bailyn, *The Ideological Origins of the American Revolution* (Cambridge: Harvard University Press, 1982), especially pp. 27–28. On Locke and Coke, see Edward S. Corwin, *The "Higher Law" Background of American Constitutionalism* (Ithaca, N.Y.: Cornell University Press, 1979). On Blackstone's teaching on "natural law" and his influence on the Founders, see W. A. Mell, "James Wilson, Alexander Hamilton, and William Blackstone," doctoral dissertation, University of Oregon, 1976 (reprinted by University Microfilms, Ann Arbor, Mich., 1980).

defining individual rights were binding on all political actors, including popular majorities and legislatures.

Most importantly for the argument at hand, in the period of the revolution, the "higher law," or natural moral law, was held to embody judicially enforceable limits on legislatures and positive law. Coke, whose *Commentaries* Jefferson called "the universal law-book of students," argued that "when an act of Parliament is against common right and reason, or repugnant, or impossible to be performed, the common law will control it and adjudge such act to be void."[78]

John Locke, the political thinker who exercised the greatest influence on the republic's founding generation, argued that men gave up none of their natural rights when entering political society; they gave to government only the power to better "preserve" their natural rights to "liberty and property."[79] Thomas Jefferson echoed Lockean theory when, in 1816, he asserted,

> Our legislators are not sufficiently apprised of the rightful limits of their power; that their true office is to declare and enforce only our natural rights and duties, and to take none of them from us. . . . When the laws have declared and enforced all this, they have fulfilled their functions; and the idea is quite unfounded that on entering society we give up any natural right.[80]

Not all the Founders adhered strictly, even in theory, to Lockeanism, and none of them acted solely on the basis of morality. Prudence, together with forms of political wisdom beyond moral reflection, comes into play in any successful act of statecraft. These facts notwithstanding, it is safe to say that the Founders did not doubt the existence of moral rights that bind popular governments. The Constitution itself, moreover, does not confer rights, but only "secures" them. And the Ninth Amendment explicitly calls upon constitutional interpreters not to "deny or disparage" the existence of rights not stated explicitly in the Constitution. By implication, then, the Constitution calls upon all citizens and public officials to reflect upon the rights that people have even in the absence of explicit political acknowledgment. The Ninth Amendment calls upon

[78]Corwin, p. 42.

[79]John Locke, *Two Treatises on Government*, Second Treatise, ed. Peter Laslett (New York: New American Library, 1965) par. 131, pp. 398–99.

[80]Thomas Jefferson, as quoted in Murphy, "Art," p. 140.

conscientious interpreters to reflect upon natural rights and so to engage in moral theory.

The New Right's moral skepticism, as well as its disparaging attitude toward rights not explicitly stated in the text of the Constitution, find little support in the ideas of the Founders or in the text of the Constitution. Not surprisingly, then, judicially enforceable moral principles, even those not explicitly stated in the Constitution, have played an important role throughout U.S. history. Early on, Justice Chase invoked, in *Calder* v. *Bull*, "the general principles of law and reason" that constrain legislators even in the absence of explicit constitutional provisions.[81]

Chief Justice Marshall, an ardent nationalist, could have struck down Georgia's revocation of a land grant in *Fletcher* v. *Peck* by invoking only the Constitution's contracts clause. Instead, he went beyond the text of the Constitution and engaged in a considerable discussion of "the great principles of justice, whose authority is universally acknowledged."[82] Seventeen years later, in *Ogden* v. *Saunders*, Marshall invoked the "abstract philosophy" of natural rights: "Individuals do not derive from government their right to contract, but bring that right with them into society. . . . [E]very man retains [the right] to acquire property, to dispose of that property according to his own judgment, and to pledge himself for a future act."[83]

When one thinks of the American political tradition at its best, Abraham Lincoln must rank alongside the greatest of the Founders. Lincoln's political morality, his central concern with human equality as a moral principle, stands sharply at odds with Bork's skepticism. In the Gettysburg Address, Lincoln described the central proposition of the Declaration of Independence, to which the nation was dedicated at its birth, as "an abstract truth applicable to all men and all times." Lincoln, unlike Bork, held that right and wrong depend on standards of judgment independent of mere opinion. What Lincoln would have thought of the assertion that the gratifications of slave traders and slaves, for instance, are not morally distinguishable, or are distinguishable only quantitatively, may easily be inferred from his Peoria speech of 1854:

[81]3 Dall. 395 (1798).
[82]3 L.Ed. 162 (1810).
[83]2 Wheaton 213 (1827).

All these free blacks are the descendants of slaves, or have been slaves themselves, and they would be now, but for *something* which has operated on their white owners, inducing them, at vast pecuniary sacrifices, to liberate them. What is that *something*? Is there any mistaking it? In all these cases it is your sense of justice, and human sympathy, continually telling you, that the poor negro has some natural right to himself—that those who deny it, and make merchandise of him, deserve kicking, contempt, and death.[84]

After the Civil War, the development of the doctrine of "substantive due process" carried forward the "higher law" tradition in the form of judicially protected economic liberties. Accordingly, Bork's disparaging attitude toward moral rights neglects not only the ideas of the Framers but also important aspects of the American constitutional and political tradition.

Bork is on firmer ground when he charges that in recent times the Supreme Court, in defining values sufficiently "fundamental" to warrant judicial protection, has neglected some rights, especially economic ones, for no good reason. In this way, the Court has indeed been "political"; it has ignored the high standing of economic rights in the Constitution's text, in our political tradition, and in moral theory. The modern Court has erected a constitutional double standard by giving high place to "personal rights" while neglecting economic rights that are at least as well founded in the Constitution.

The Supreme Court can and should be criticized for the narrow way in which it has defined those "fundamental" values and "preferred" freedoms worthy of judicial protection. It should not be concluded, however, that the active judicial defense of liberty and rights should be abandoned, for this defense is supported by the Constitution's text, by the ideas of the Framers, and by our political tradition. The proper course, it seems, is for conscientious interpreters of the Constitution to correct, not abandon, judicial activism.

There is clearly a close fit between the three levels of the New

[84]Abraham Lincoln, speech delivered at Peoria, Ill., 1854, as quoted in Harry V. Jaffa, *Crisis of the House Divided* (Seattle: University of Washington Press, 1973), p. 312. For a discussion of Lincoln's view of the moral status of the Declaration of Independence, see Jaffa, chap. 14; and Gary J. Jacobsohn, "Abraham Lincoln 'On this Question of Judicial Authority': The Theory of Constitutional Aspiration," *Western Political Quarterly* 36, no. 1 (1983): 52–70.

Right's jurisprudence. The resort to historical intentions to construe rights narrowly is supported by the preference for majority power over individual liberty, and that in turn is supported by moral skepticism. And yet at each level, the New Right's position is diametrically opposed to the ideas of the Framers, to the text of the Constitution, and to morality itself, which limits and defines our ultimate political duties. Having proceeded thus far in the task of clearing the ground, it is now worthwhile to consider briefly the possible form of a principled judicial activism.

V. Principled Judicial Activism

Assuming the preceding critique of the jurisprudence of the New Right is sound, there is a need for a constitutional vision with a robust conception of judicially enforceable rights grounded in the text of the Constitution, in sound moral thinking, and in our political tradition. A principled judicial activism would overcome the incoherence of the modern Court's double standard.

A principled jurisprudence would draw upon all the sources available and relevant to the task of constitutional interpretation. First and foremost among these sources are the text and structure of the Constitution and the nature of the institutions established by the document. However, both the text, especially the preamble (which Lino Graglia dismisses as a mere "rhetorical flourish"[85]) and the Ninth Amendment, and our tradition direct us beyond the rights explicitly stated in the document, so it is not possible to dispense with an understanding of the morality of individual rights. For the conscientious interpreter, moral theory is an aid to, not a substitute for, interpretation of the text. Given the openness of the text to a morality of broad individual rights, the two are complementary rather than competing, and our moral duties and our duties as citizens overlap. (Robert Bork once advocated roughly the kind of principled activism being advanced here; he allowed that a "legitimate judicial activism" would give "content to the concept of natural rights in a case-by-case interpretation of the Constitution."[86])

The jurisprudence of the modern Supreme Court has developed in response to the perceived illegitimacy of the Court's efforts, over many years, to develop principled ways of limiting the regulatory powers of the federal and state governments in the economic sphere. The Court's efforts in the economic sphere were directed at imposing limits on Congress's regulatory powers under the commerce

[85]Graglia, "Would the Court," p. 815.
[86]See Robert H. Bork, "The Supreme Court Needs a New Philosophy," *Fortune* 78 (December 1968): 138 ff.

clause and at defining individual economic liberties enforceable against the states under the Fourteenth Amendment's due process clause. Despite the fact that most constitutional scholars on both the left and the right now argue that the Court should give Congress and the states a free hand in the economic sphere, the Court's efforts, while far from perfect, were on the whole legitimate and principled exercises in constitutional interpretation. (Richard Epstein, Bernard Siegan, and Martin Schapiro are exceptions to the overwhelming, but I believe ill-founded, consensus on this point.[87])

In the late 19th and early 20th centuries, the Court forged distinctions to define and limit Congress's power to "regulate Commerce . . . among the several States."[88] Of particular importance was the distinction made between commerce and production that placed regulation of production beyond Congress's power and among the reserved powers of the states.[89] These distinctions were swept away when the Court moved to accept the constitutionality of the New Deal.[90] However, any conscientious interpreter of the Constitution must feel uncomfortable with a commerce power so extensive that it sacrifices other values with high constitutional standing, or with a commerce power used pretextually to pursue ends unrelated to commerce.[91]

Consider the case of an Ohio farmer named Filburn who sowed 23 acres of wheat wholly for consumption on his farm. He was fined by Franklin Roosevelt's Department of Agriculture, however, for harvesting in excess of his quota, which the department had set at 11.1 acres.[92] The New Deal's Agricultural Adjustment Act of 1938

[87]For a lengthy analysis of the relevant case law, see Bernard Siegan, *Economic Liberties and the Constitution* (Chicago: University of Chicago, 1980). See also Martin Schapiro, "The Constitution and Economic Liberties," in Harmon, *Essays*, pp. 74–98. An important addition to this literature is Richard Epstein, *Takings: Private Property and the Power of Eminent Domain* (Cambridge: Harvard University Press, 1985).

[88]U.S. Constitution, Article I, section 8.

[89]*U.S. v. E. C. Knight*, 156 U.S. 1 (1895).

[90]See *N.L.R.B. v. Jones & Laughlin Steel Co.*, 301 U.S. 1 (1937); and *U.S. v. Darby*, 312 U.S. 100 (1941).

[91]For a pretextual use of the commerce power to suppress lotteries and thereby pursue an end subsumed by the states' reserved police powers, see *Champion v. Ames*, 188 U.S. 321 (1903). For the apparent abandonment of Marshall's pretextual limitation, forged in *McCulloch*, see *U.S. v. Darby*, 312 U.S. 100 (1941).

[92]*Wickard v. Filburn*, 317 U.S. 111 (1942).

gave the secretary of agriculture the power to establish such quotas to help regulate supply and stabilize prices. Although there was no "commerce" involved in Filburn's activity, the Court ruled in *Wickard* v. *Filburn* that his activities "affected commerce" and that excess supply constituted an "obstruction to commerce."[93]

The problem with *Wickard*, of course, is that it sacrifices property rights closely bound up with personal autonomy to a policy rather loosely related to Congress's commerce power. Long before, Justice Holmes had warned, in *Northern Securities Co.* v. *U.S.*, that the logic of indirect effects on a "national market" had no limit: "Almost anything—marriage, birth, death, may in some manner affect commerce."[94] However, without the sorts of defining and limiting distinctions that the Court has since abandoned, it is hard to see why marriage and divorce should not fall under commercial regulation as well.

Besides the limits placed on the commerce power, the old Court also deployed against the states the doctrine of "substantive due process," a doctrine now identified most closely with the case of *Lochner* v. *New York*.[95] In *Lochner*, the Court struck down a New York statute limiting the working hours of bakery employees as an abridgment of "liberty of contract." The modern Court has not abandoned the idea that the Fourteenth Amendment, which says, "No State shall . . . deprive any person of life, liberty, or property without due process of law," implies that there are substantive limits on the ways in which the state can interfere with private relations. The Court has simply shifted its inquiries away from the economic sphere. When it comes to state economic regulation, the Court requires nothing more than the merest "rationality" to justify restrictions on individual liberty. In instances when legislators have not put forward a rational basis for restrictions on economic liberty, the Court has simply hypothesized its own rationale, as in *Williamson* v. *Lee Optical* and *Ferguson* v. *Skrupka*.[96]

The modern Court has largely abandoned the protection of substantive economic values, but it has not abandoned fundamental values altogether. The Court closely scrutinizes legislation touching on a list of "preferred freedoms," such as the right to freedom of

[93]Ibid.
[94]193 U.S. 197 (1904).
[95]198 U.S. 45 (1905).
[96]348 U.S. 343 (1955) and 372 U.S. 726 (1963), respectively.

speech, of religion, and of the press, and more recently the right to privacy and the equal protection of the laws.

The Constitution, as already noted, manifests a basic concern with protecting a wide range of human freedoms. Government powers are limited, and the Ninth Amendment explicitly states that people have rights not explicitly mentioned in the document. Judges cannot flinch, therefore, at the task of applying the same expansive logic to individual rights that *McCulloch* applies to government powers. An excellent case in point is *Griswold* v. *Connecticut,* which Bork derides as an arbitrary judicial creation of a new right.[97] *Griswold* struck down a Connecticut statute that made it illegal for married couples to use contraceptives. The Court based its decision on an implicit constitutional right to zones of privacy, which emanate from, or form "penumbras" around, the specific guarantees of the Bill of Rights. As Justice Douglas argued, these implicit, penumbral rights, including one protecting the privacy of the marriage relationship, help give life and substance to express guarantees:

> Various guarantees create zones of privacy. The right of association contained in the penumbra of the First Amendment is one, as we have seen. The Third Amendment in its protection against the quartering of soldiers "in any house" in time of peace without the consent of the owner is another facet of that privacy. The Fourth Amendment explicitly affirms the "right of the people to be secure in their persons, houses, papers, and effects against unreasonable searches and seizures." The Fifth Amendment in its Self-Incrimination Clause enables the citizen to create a zone of privacy which government may not force him to surrender to his detriment.

Justice Goldberg, concurring, emphasized the importance of taking the Ninth Amendment seriously: "The Ninth Amendment shows a belief of the Constitution's authors that fundamental rights exist that are not expressly enumerated in the first eight amendments. . . . [T]he subsequently enacted 14th Amendment prohibits the states as well from abridging fundamental personal liberties."

Most commentators on the left applaud the Court's shift from protecting economic values to protecting noneconomic ones such as privacy. Conservatives like Bork, on the other hand, see the new

[97]381 U.S. 479 (1965).

jurisprudence as no better than the old. Conservatives want the Court to abandon the protection of not only economic liberties but of all "fundamental" interests or "substantive" values other than those explicitly stated in the constitutional text and originally intended by the Framers.

In a sense, the conservatives do have a point, for both the new "activist" jurisprudence and the old are flawed. In both cases, the choice of values to be protected is partial, unprincipled, and, therefore, political. The "Old Men," as the justices supporting the majority position in the *Lochner*-era Court were known, failed to adequately recognize the high place that the Constitution gives to such noneconomic liberties as freedom of speech.[98] The modern Court errs, likewise, in arbitrarily neglecting values that have a high place in the Constitution's scheme of values. Nevertheless, these errors can be corrected without abandoning the active judicial protection of individual rights. The error in both cases is not that constitutionally protected liberties are judicially enforced, but that not all constitutionally protected liberties are enforced. Worse than the application of the double standard would be to suppose, as does Bork, that American citizens have no judicially enforceable rights except those explicitly stated in the Constitution and specifically intended by the Framers.

The modern Court's double standard, which neglects economic liberties and protects other "personal" liberties, like privacy, is incoherent and untenable. It flies in the face of the plain words of the Constitution, ignores important aspects of our legal and political traditions, and fails to recognize that economic and other "favored" liberties are mutually interdependent and commonly grounded on an even more basic, implicit constitutional principle: the dignity of persons who are bearers of broad rights and capable of responsible self-government.

The underlying logic of *Griswold* is essentially correct, though Douglas's execution leaves much to be desired. Just as *McCulloch* sought to interpret and enforce the principles and purposes underlying the Constitution's enumeration of Congress's powers, so *Griswold* seeks to enforce the principles and purposes underlying the Constitution's specific guarantees of rights. Conscientious interpreters cannot shirk either the project of *McCulloch* or the project

[98]See, among other cases, *Schenck* v. *U.S.*, 249 U.S. 47 (1919); *Abrams* v. *U.S.*, 250 U.S. 616 (1919); and *Whitney* v. *California*, 274 U.S. 357 (1927).

of *Griswold*. From specific textual provisions, structures, and underlying purposes, conscientious interpreters must strive toward a complete and defensible theory of the Constitution as the best means to achieve our best understanding of its great ends: "to form a more perfect Union, establish Justice, insure domestic Tranquility, provide for the common defence, promote the general Welfare, and secure the Blessings of Liberty to ourselves and our Posterity." Only by fusing constitutional and moral theory can interpreters at once vindicate and justify the Constitution's authority as supreme law; only in this way do interpreters help insure that our republic will remain worthy of allegiance and that we will be governed by more than power and mere willfullness.

Constitutional commentators on and off the bench are coming to recognize that the new double standard is no better than the old. They perceive that what is needed is a jurisprudence that acknowledges the constitutional status of both economic and other important liberties. As Justice Stewart pointed out in *Lynch* v. *Household Finance Corporation*:

> The dichotomy between personal liberties and property rights is a false one. Property does not have rights. People have rights. The right to enjoy property without unlawful deprivation, no less than the right to speak out or the right to travel, is, in truth, a "personal" right. . . . [A] fundamental interdependence exists between the personal right to liberty and the personal right in property. Neither could have meaning without the other. That rights in property are basic civil rights has long been recognized.[99]

Although the Court of the *Lochner* era may justly be accused of inadequate concern with noneconomic freedoms, it did take the important step of holding that the word "liberty" in the Fourteenth Amendment's due process clause includes the liberty of speech.[100] Even the crustiest of the "Old Men," Justice McReynolds, recognized the close relation between economic and other personal liberties and thus pointed the way toward a principled synthesis. In *Meyer* v. *Nebraska*, the Court overturned the conviction of a German-language teacher under a statute prohibiting the teaching of foreign

---

[99]405 U.S. 538, 552 (1972). Stewart cites Locke, John Adams, and Blackstone on this point.

[100]*Gitlow* v. *New York*, 268 U.S. 652 (1925).

languages to young children.[101] Justice McReynolds articulated a broad conception of the liberty protected by the Fourteenth Amendment:

> Without doubt, it denotes not merely freedom from bodily restraint, but also the right of the individual to contract, to engage in any of the common occupations of life, to acquire useful knowledge, to marry, establish a home and bring up children, to worship God according to the dictates of his conscience, and generally to enjoy those privileges long recognized at common law as essential to the orderly pursuit of happiness by free men.[102]

McReynolds correctly linked the autonomy and intellectual freedom of parents and students with the "economic" right of language teachers to pursue their calling.[103]

More recently, in *Moore* v. *East Cleveland*, a city zoning ordinance limiting occupancy of dwellings to a single, "nuclear" family was successfully challenged by a grandmother living with her two grandchildren.[104] In his plurality opinion, Justice Powell argued from the traditional importance of autonomous family life, and he denied the state's authority to require "all to live in certain narrowly defined family patterns." Justice Stevens's concurring opinion explicitly linked the values at stake with the grandmother's property rights, in particular her common-law right to decide who resides on her property. He found no substantial relation between the ordinance and the state's police powers to regulate health, safety, and morals. By placing the act beyond the state's legitimate powers, Stevens found it a "taking" of property without just compensation or due process.

Bork, as noted later in this discussion, charges that a political regime that elevates respect for individual rights to a constitutional command sacrifices the community's public morality to moral relativism. In fact, respecting the whole range of human rights, including property rights, is the best way for a pluralistic society such as ours to express a public morality.

A recent Michigan case highlights the deep interdependence of property rights and the secure enjoyment of liberties associated

[101]262 U.S. 390 (1923).
[102]262 U.S. 399 (1923).
[103]See also *Pierce* v. *Society of Sisters*, 268 U.S. 510 (1925).
[104]431 U.S. 494 (1977).

with self-determination, or autonomy, and community. *Poletown Neighborhood Council* v. *City of Detroit* arose over the taking by eminent domain of an entire Detroit neighborhood that the General Motors Corporation wanted to raze for the construction of an automobile plant.[105] The Michigan Supreme Court refused to step in and protect the property owners in this ethnic working-class neighborhood despite state and federal constitutional requirements that land be taken only for "public use." Construing government powers broadly and individual rights narrowly, as Bork recommends, the Michigan Supreme Court said the Constitution would be satisfied because the seizure and transfer to General Motors would provide a "public benefit." However, if property rights are to count for so little in the face of a government pursuing policy ends, then families, communities, and the other traditional groups of which the New Right is so solicitous are all rendered insecure and vulnerable to political vagaries and the passions of the moment.

The New Right rejoinder to the argument for combining protections for a broad sphere of individual liberties, both economic and otherwise, would undoubtedly be that one should not combine both sorts of protections but reject both. The conservative strategy does avoid a constitutional and moral double standard, but at the expense of a total blindness to the constitutional status of a broad expanse of individual liberty.

One final New Right challenge to an individual rights-centered jurisprudence remains to be taken up: consideration of the claim that a polity that gives its highest allegiance to individual rights surrenders to moral relativism and abandons the possibility of realizing in its political practices a form of moral community.

---

[105]410 Mich. 616, 304 N.W. 2d 455 (1981).

50

VI. Liberty and Community

The broadly rights-based jurisprudence outlined in the preceding section is open to an important line of criticism. Bork and other figures of the New Right have put forward a version of what may be called the communitarian critique of liberal politics. Bork claims that judges who actively defend individual rights are moved by "extra-constitutional moral and political notions" to substitute "moral relativism" for a common morality.[106] However, does a central constitutional concern with individual rights represent the abandonment of a common or public morality?

Bork explains his opposition to what he calls the "privatization of morality" in terms that have been repeated and paraphrased by Attorney General Meese:

> As Lord Devlin said, "What makes a society is a community of ideas, not political ideas alone but also ideas about the way its members should behave and govern their lives." A society that ceases to be a community increases the danger that weariness with turmoil and relativism may bring about an order in which many more, and more valuable, freedoms are lost than those we thought we were protecting.[107]

Terry Eastland, special assistant to Meese, worries about the triumph of a "culture of rights" in an America

> so awash in rights that we are virtually unable to pass legislation reflecting traditional religious and moral views. Moral relativism will then be the rule, at law; and what is true at law will shape what is practiced. For when morality is strictly up to the individual, with no judgment possible by communities, it is likely that everyone will do what is right in his own eyes. . . . America will then become a land composed of strangers whose religion, if any,

---

[106]Bork, *Tradition*, p. 3.

[107]Ibid., p. 4; also quoted in part and paraphrased in part by Meese, AEI address, pp. 10–11.

is a private matter, and who are bound by no social ties or common aspirations.[108]

Contrary to the views of "liberal" justices, the New Right would allow legislatures to enforce the majority's view of good conduct in spheres often considered private. Bork rejects the idea that "individuals are entitled to their moral beliefs but may not gather as a community to express those beliefs as law."[109] He would treat violations of the majority's view of good conduct as "moral harms" against the community at large—harms to be treated as "pollution" to the moral "atmosphere." The New Right rejects the old idea that individuals should be free to live as they choose as long as they respect the equal freedom of others. For Bork, the "major freedom, of our kind of society is the freedom to choose to have a public morality."[110]

To shield the power of a moral majority from judicial interventions on behalf of individual rights, Bork distinguishes between what he calls the "common sense of the community," which include its practices and traditions, and "abstract and philosophical" arguments, such as the "universalistic style of legal thought" propounded by "theorists of moral abstraction."[111] Bork wishes to vest political authority in the "common sense of the people," that is, in a common sense untutored by philosophy and unrestrained by reflection. Individual rights, which shield people in their private conduct from the meddling of others, are treated by the New Right as obstacles to the majority's power to impose a single and exacting code of conduct on all.

Just how one would go about reconciling Bork's moral skepticism with his concern to promote a "public morality" is not clear. But neither is it clear, as noted above, how this skepticism can be squared with the apparently principled preference for majoritarianism. (Without a principle of moral equality, why should one prefer the "gratifications" of the majority to those of a minority?) Nor is it at all obvious that the majority's right to rule is any less abstract than the individual rights to liberty that Bork dismisses as

---

[108]Terry Eastland, "The Politics of Morality and Religion: A Primer," in *Whose Values?* ed. Carl Horn (Ann Arbor, Mich.: Servant Books, 1985), p. 17.

[109]Bork, *Tradition*, p. 3.

[110]Ibid., p. 9.

[111]Ibid., pp. 7–11.

"too abstract." To seek logical coherence in Bork's position is fruitless; its coherence is rhetorical rather than logical.

What is clear is that the New Right errs in identifying individual rights with moral relativism. The liberal norms that underlie individual rights embody a public morality, and this liberal public morality comports with the Constitution and tradition and moral reasons more substantial than any advanced by the New Right.

The individual rights-centered public morality has another virtue lacking in the intolerant morality of the New Right: it is morally defensible in a vast, heterogeneous republic such as the United States, in which people differ widely about their religious beliefs, lifestyles, goals, and commitments. The relevant question is not whether America is to be a moral community, but what kind of community it is to be. The important question is whether America should be an open, tolerant community that respects liberty, individuality, and diversity.

The political supremacy of a conception of justice centered on the value of liberty and individual rights forms the core of the tradition of liberal individualism. And the term "liberal" is taken here to refer not to the narrow contemporary sense that marks off the left side of the American political spectrum but to the older and broader sense of the term, represented centrally by such figures as John Locke and John Stuart Mill and the founders of the American republic.[112]

To recognize the moral force of individuality is to recognize that intelligent, responsible persons can and do pursue widely divergent personal goals and projects. This observation is especially true in a vast, diverse nation such as the United States. This "extended republic" embraces a vast populace with a dizzying variety of faiths, cultures, goals, and lifestyles. Liberalism stands for the conviction that each person has a basic duty to respect the rights of others.

[112]Bork refers dismissively to Mill's classic *On Liberty*. (See Bork, *Tradition*, p. 5.) It should be noted here that liberal thought is now split between adherents to classical liberalism (or libertarianism) and proponents of contemporary (or egalitarian) liberalism. All liberals share the values being defended in this discussion against Bork's conservatism: the basic right of all persons to choose how to live—to devise, pursue, and revise a plan of life within the bounds set by the equal freedom of others. But the concern with both economic and noneconomic rights is typical only of classical liberalism. Contemporary liberals tend to downgrade economic rights in favor of income redistribution; they support the modern variant of the double standard discussed in chapter 5.

Liberals hold that people derive their common dignity and equal right to liberty not from any particular allegiance to nation, class, sect, or caste, but from their capacity to reflect and understand, to choose and act and be held responsible, to settle on projects and pursue them, to change their minds and begin again, and to restrain their desires and the pursuit of their goals when other people's rights are at stake.

French sociologist Émile Durkheim well understood that liberal individualism represents not the abandonment of public values or of community but the embrace of a substantive moral vision that accords with a people's diversity. It is worth quoting Durkheim at some length:

> Doubtless if the dignity of the individual derived from his individual qualities, or from those particular characteristics which distinguish him from others, one might fear that he would become enclosed in a sort of moral egoism that would render all social cohesion impossible. But in reality he receives his dignity from a higher source, one which he shares with all men. . . . It is humanity that is sacred and worthy of respect. And this is not his exclusive possession. It is distributed among his fellows, and in consequence he cannot take it as a goal for his conduct without being obliged to go beyond himself and turn toward others. . . . Impersonal and anonymous, such an end soars above all particular consciences and can thus serve as a rallying point for them. . . . All that societies require in order to hold together is that their members fix their eyes on the same end and come together in a single faith. . . . [I]ndividualism thus understood is not the glorification of the self, but of the individual in general. Its motive force is not egoism but sympathy for all that is human, a wider pity for all sufferings, for all human miseries, a more ardent desire to combat and alleviate them, a greater thirst for justice. Is this not the way to achieve a community of all men of good will?[113]

Liberal citizens recognize that their rights are grounded in principles and values that protect individualism in general. Liberal principles are based not on self-love but on respect for diversity, plurality, and the dignity of beings with the capacity for reflective and responsible choice. In this way, liberal individualism becomes

[113]Émile Durkheim, "Individualism and the Intellectuals," trans. and intro. Steven Lukes, *Political Studies* 17, no. 1 (1969): 23–24.

a moral commitment, a commitment embodying general, impersonal concerns and values that overarch and subordinate self-centeredness. Thus understood, individual liberty provides the foundation for a public morality, a moral community.

The supremacy of the Constitution embodies liberalism's ultimate commitment to moral standards. The Constitution, properly interpreted, embodies not simply the will of some authoritative group but standards of justice and respect for the full gamut of moral rights. Bork, however, would deny this moral status to the Constitution. He continually emphasizes that judges owe their allegiance to the will of the Framers (in the form of specific historical intentions) or to the will of the majority. And in the place of rights, justice, and morality, he believes only in the gratifications and preferences of the greatest number. This moral cynicism devalues the status of the Constitution and cheapens the currency of our political discourse; it also undermines the possibility of a moral community in America.

It is surely unrealistic to expect that the citizens of this diverse nation will ever settle on a single vision of the good life. We can neither hope nor expect that one such vision will ever secure the allegiance of Jerry Falwell and Jane Fonda, of urban yuppies and suburban families, of Midwestern farmers and Vietnamese immigrants. To grant supreme political status to the preferences of the greatest number, rather than to public moral norms protecting the equal liberty of all, constitutes oppression and invites social conflict.

Individuals prize rights not because they wish to live in isolation but because they want to choose with whom to associate, in what manner, and for what purpose. After all, people's disagreements about personal preferences and lifestyles are as wide and deep as their differences over religious beliefs. To require all to live according to one set of ideals, one vision of the good life, would be to turn back the clock to the era of religious civil wars following the Reformation. It would indeed be ironic if Americans, descendants of those who sought to establish a haven from religious persecution, abandoned liberal toleration, liberal peace, and liberal justice for the spurious traditionalism of the New Right.

Community ends with coercion; it doesn't begin there. And a community cannot be a moral community unless it is also a free community. The rights that define associative freedoms, and those that provide for autonomy and personal security, are part of the constitution of any good community. They are part of what makes community valuable. And so individual rights, far from being corrosive of community as the New Right charges, are constitutive components of America's liberal, constitutional community.

VII. Conclusion

The central pillars of the jurisprudence of the New Right crumble when subjected to scrutiny. The Jurisprudence of Original Intent raises a host of apparently insoluble problems, and it ends in self-destruction when it becomes evident that the Framers did not intend the republic to be guided by their specific historical intentions. Historical intentions, in any case, are invoked selectively rather than consistently by the conservatives as a means of advancing a majoritarian political program that itself is deeply at odds with the text and spirit of the Constitution, the ideas of the Founders, and much of our political tradition. The New Right's majoritarianism is serviced not only by the selective invocation of original intentions but also by the selective invocation of moral skepticism: the cynical acid that is meant to dissolve "abstract" individual rights is never applied to the majority's purported right to rule. And yet, as pointed out here, unless one inserts an "abstract" premise of moral equality, there is no reason to prefer the gratifications of the majority to those of the minority.

Moral skepticism, like intentionalism and majoritarianism, is more than extraneous to the Constitution; it is positively at odds with the founding document, the Declaration of Independence, the ideas of the Founders, and the moral aspirations of Americans at their best. The New Right fails to recognize, finally, that individual rights are supportive both of community and morality. In dismissing individual liberty and rights as "relativistic" and corrosive of moral community, the New Right undermines the political morality that the Constitution itself embodies.

The jurisprudence of the New Right creates a moral void at the heart of the Constitution. Bork and others see a community concerned with rights as one whose members are drifting apart, growing weary "with turmoil and relativism," and becoming "strangers" to one another.[114] The point of this exercise, for at least some on the New Right, is clear enough. They wish to fill the moral vacuum

[114]Bork, *Tradition*, p. 4; Eastland, p. 72.

they establish in liberal constitutionalism with religious values, specifically with Christian values. As Terry Eastland puts it:

> Protestant Christianity . . . tutored the first generations of Americans. It provided what we today would call the value system of the society. . . . Christianity provided an attitude toward law that law itself could not provide. It instilled in Americans the civic virtues of respect for legitimate authority and obedience to it. By strengthening the legal order, Christianity in turn strengthened the social order and thus the bonds of community from which emerge still other civic virtues—those of altruism, neighborliness, and patriotism.[115]

But religion is mentioned only twice in the Constitution. Just before its ratification provisions and signing, the Constitution says that "no religious Test shall ever be required as a Qualification to any Office or public Trust under the United States," and in the opening words of the First Amendment, it says that "Congress shall make no law respecting an establishment of religion, or prohibiting the free exercise thereof." The public morality embodied in the Constitution, while it surely accommodates free religious practice, does not rest on particular religious beliefs or on the presumption of religious agreement.

This essay has tried to suggest that the Constitution should not be read in terms of specific historical intentions, or as the expression of the will of some authoritative group, or as an acknowledgment of majority sovereignty. The Constitution is better read in terms of the aspirations set out in the preamble, as an attempt to, among other things, "establish Justice . . . promote the general Welfare, and secure the Blessings of Liberty to ourselves and our Posterity." The Constitution's aspirations are moral, and, when fleshed out by the interpreter, they are capable of providing the sorts of common values and ideals that may unite even a diverse community.

The ideal of community implicit in the Constitution would count tolerance, openness to change and diversity, and reflectiveness among its public virtues. Furthermore, the very practice of respecting the rights of people who lead different lives fosters liberal attitudes of broad sympathies, friendliness, and even altruism. Citizens loyal to our liberal, democratic Constitution support reasoned public deliberation and persuasion rather than force and

[115]Eastland, pp. 14–15.

arbitrary power. As conscientious interpreters, they would review the acts of public officials for conformity with the Constitution and be prepared to act in politics themselves as pursuers of constitutional ideals and not as promoters of narrow interests.[116]

One would have to be very naive or blind to claim that our current political practices realize this ideal vision of constitutional community. However, this ideal is adumbrated by the Constitution and it is far more attractive than the opposing vision advanced by the New Right. Principled judicial activism would help move us closer to this ideal.

The issues discussed in this essay are "constitutional" in the broadest and deepest sense, affecting not only the determination of court cases but also the shape of our polity and our lives as citizens. In this sense, constitutional interpretation cannot help but be political, and politics, at least at its best, cannot dispense with serious constitutional debate.

The judicial activism defended here should not be confused with judicial supremacy. Principled activism in no way implies that the Supreme Court is the final interpreter of the Constitution (except for the parties to the cases that come before it, and for inferior courts) or that Supreme Court interpretations of the Constitution are binding on Congress, the president, or the citizenry. The Constitution itself is supreme, and the members of each of the three coordinate branches of the federal government are sworn to uphold the Constitution in performing their official functions; the oaths and the coordinate status of the president and members of Congress imply that they have an obligation to interpret for themselves and not to defer to others. As President Andrew Jackson put it, "Each public officer who takes an oath to support the Constitution swears that he will support it as he understands it and not as it is understood by others."[117] Presidents Jefferson and Lincoln also argued, albeit with some variations, for a view of the three branches of the federal government as competing interpreters.[118]

Rejecting the constitutional vision of the New Right should not be confused with a wholesale rejection of conservative sentiments

[116]The present author is currently working on a longer project on the relation between liberal politics and ideals of community, virtue, and citizenship.

[117]Andrew Jackson, as quoted in John Agresto, *The Supreme Court and Constitutional Democracy* (Ithaca, N.Y.: Cornell University Press, 1984), p. 128.

[118]Agresto, chap. 5.

or of patriotism. Only a blind conservatism is without reasons for valuing what it seeks to preserve. Only an unreflective and uncritical patriotism ("my country, right or wrong") forgets that it is in aspiring to worthy principles and ideals that government, Constitution, and country become worthy of loyalty, allegiance, and self-sacrifice. Instead of the unreflective traditionalism of the New Right, we would do far better to aspire to Lincoln's eulogistic remembrance of Henry Clay, who, Lincoln said, "loved his country partly because it was his own country, but mostly because it was a free country; and he burned with a zeal for its advancement . . . because he saw in such, the advancement . . . of human liberty, human right, and human nature."[119]

[119]Pangle, p. 30.

About the Author

Stephen Macedo has accepted a position as assistant professor in the Government Department at Harvard University. He holds degrees from the London School of Economics, Oxford University, and Princeton University, and is an adjunct scholar of the Cato Institute.

Cato Institute

Founded in 1977, the Cato Institute is a public policy research foundation dedicated to broadening the parameters of policy debate to allow consideration of more options that are consistent with the traditional American principles of limited government, individual liberty, and peace. Toward that goal, the Institute strives to achieve a greater involvement of the intelligent, concerned lay public in questions of policy and the proper role of government.

The Institute is named for *Cato's Letters*, pamphlets that were widely read in the American Colonies in the early eighteenth century and played a major role in laying the philosophical foundation for the revolution that followed. Since that revolution, civil and economic liberties have been eroded as the number and complexity of social problems have grown. Today virtually no aspect of human life is free from the domination of a governing class of politico-economic interests. A pervasive intolerance for individual rights is shown by government's arbitrary intrusions into private economic transactions and its disregard for civil liberties.

To counter this trend the Cato Institute undertakes an extensive publications program dealing with the complete spectrum of policy issues. Books, monographs, and shorter studies are commissioned to examine the federal budget, Social Security, regulation, NATO, international trade, and a myriad of other issues. Major policy conferences are held throughout the year, from which papers are published thrice yearly in the *Cato Journal*.

In order to maintain an independent posture, the Cato Institute accepts no government funding. Contributions are received from foundations, corporations, and individuals, and other revenue is generated from the sale of publications. The Institute is a nonprofit, tax-exempt, educational foundation under Section 501(c)3 of the Internal Revenue Code.

CATO INSTITUTE
224 Second St., S.E.
Washington, D.C. 20003